MW01267951

Katrina After the Storm

VOLUNTEERING IN AMERICA, AN INSIDE VIEW

By Annette Ladowitz, LCSW

CLEMSON HOUSE PUBLISHING
CALIFORNIA

Copyright © 2006 Annette Ladowitz

Printed in the United States of America
by Gorham Printing, Rochester, Washington

Cover design by David Ladowitz

Editing by B. J. Fandrich

The names of the residents in the shelters have all been changed.

ISBN-10: 0-9785962-0-X
ISBN-13: 978-0-9785962-0-0

FIRST EDITION

Clemson House
Publishing

This book is dedicated to those who lost so much,
to those who volunteered, and to those who made
contributions so that reaching out was possible.

Contents

    Work the Crowd

    Paper Clips

    Jay and His Family

    The Scream

    He's Just a Spoiled Brat

    The Wild Ride

    Changing of the Guard

Acknowledgments

TO MY HUSBAND, Steve, for teaching me how to be silly and to laugh every day. Your wonderful sense of humor has carried me through this process. To my daughter, Michelle, for her willingness to provide honest critique and for being the first to do so; and to my son, David, for tech support morning, noon, and night, for general patience in answering endless questions about how to use a new computer, and for designing the wonderful cover.

To Glenn and Cyndy Thomas who have encouraged and guided me through the publishing process.

To Vickie Powell, my supervisor at the Santa Clara County Red Cross, for allowing me to go to Louisiana and for being the first to suggest writing about it. To my fantastic Red Cross supervisor Sheldon, for providing such a refreshing and wonderful model of how to take charge without having to be in charge. To my other supervisors Debbie and Judy, for their warmth, acceptance, and understanding; to my great colleague Susan, who shared five days of getting lost with humor and who demonstrated compassion to all those she was with.

To my coworkers at my previous job and to Tierney Lynch, for managing fundraising for the Red Cross in my absence, and Sandy Hietala for reading the first chapters of this work and encouraging me to continue. To the San Jose Rotary Club, for being an inspiration with their fundraising ability and for finding a town in the South to help rebuild; to my family, neighbors, and editor, Barbara.

Most of all, to the numerous people in Louisiana whose names I don't know, some who just stopped by to say thanks, and to those who allowed me into their lives in such a personal way. I thank you all for this phenomenal opportunity to be a part of your lives. I have truly been touched by your willingness to be so genuine and giving, especially when you had lost so much. In a world that is too often filled with negative news, you provided welcome models of humanity, of what is right in this world, and what we can all strive for in difficult times. I thank you all.

Introduction

AS A WOMAN who has been happily married for thirty-six years, with two terrific grown children, I have been fortunate in life. My husband and I live in a wonderful home in a quiet, safe, and friendly neighborhood. Steve and I both live and work near home. Sometimes we meet for lunch.

I worked as a waitress when I put myself through school; taught in junior high; worked in business; and served as a social worker for more than twenty years. Jobs have always been easy to find. I've volunteered in several community organizations and have been able to travel to Mexico, Guatemala, France, England, and many other countries over the years. It has been a good life.

I've always battled with weight control and have absolutely no athletic ability. I was one of those slightly chubby kids who were the last chosen to be on a team all through school. Scuba or sky diving, white water rafting, mountain climbing, and walking on hot coals with bare feet have as much appeal to me as undergoing a root canal or liposuction. In my spare time I love to cook, garden, grow fresh vegetables, and bring flowers to work to share with coworkers.

Now, as I faced retirement, I wondered what else there was. I was looking for something different and meaningful to do. This is the story of how I found new direction, purpose, and meaning in life through the experience of going to Louisiana as a Red Cross volunteer to help with the aftermath of the Hurricane Katrina disaster.

This is the story of how ten days spent in Louisiana unfolded day by day. It is the story of how a terrible time in history provided the spark for me to get involved in life in a new way. It provided inspiration to reach out to others and tap into new energy. It reminded me that aging is a positive thing, that it brings new freedom with many new meaningful possibilities. It was a reminder that one does not have to shatter any athletic, academic, or financial records to be productive and love life. It is a reminder that happiness is not dependent upon having one's picture on the front cover of *Time Magazine*, winning the lottery, or having throngs of people clamoring for an autograph. It is a reminder that joy is found in small, everyday occurrences through sharing, giving, and receiving.

One of the goals of writing this book is the hope that by sharing my experience it may help to dispel some of our cultural biases about aging and about what we are capable of achieving. I hope it will help create a spark and inspiration so that we all reach for what we want to do in life and not let ourselves be held back by what others think we can or should accomplish. It is about what I now understand is crucial to a good, meaningful life. If I die today I will be happy in knowing I am finally seeing what is important and reaching for it every day. We do not have yesterday or tomorrow, we have only today. This is the best time of my life.

Chapter 1

The Best Vacation Ever

IT IS THE end of August 2005. I count the days accumulated for vacation. There are almost five days—one week of vacation. The days will be spent in October visiting with family and seeing my daughter, Michelle, in Pennsylvania. She is finishing a degree at Temple University, and I miss her. I think about what I will wear. Nothing fits.

It is evening and the news has been carrying a story about a hurricane off the coast near Florida. It seems typical of so many hurricanes. I turn off the evening news and go to sleep thinking about how I can lose fifteen pounds to fit into that purple size two dress.

Tomorrow night, again after work, the news is about the hurricane. People are being told to leave their homes. The TV shows some people who decide to stay. They've been through this many times before and have "ridden it out." It doesn't seem serious to me. We live in California. I go to bed early and think I will never fit into that dress again.

Once more it is evening. I'm tired and need to sleep to be ready for work tomorrow. I decide to watch TV in bed. As I watch I think this news can't be real. There are now floods, there are people standing on roof tops waiting for helicopters to rescue them. There is news about the Superdome being used for a shelter. At least people are safe, I think.

The days go by and the news is unbelievable. Each day is worse. This cannot be here in the United States! There is no food, no water. People are looting. It is wrong. It looks like pictures out of Africa. How can this be happening here? It is New Orleans, Louisiana, USA. I wonder what I would do if our children, Michelle and David, were still infants and we had no milk. Wouldn't Steve and I risk jail to feed our children? Some looters are feeding their neighbors. These are "criminal acts" and I wonder how we define criminality.

It is day three or four of watching the news. By now people are in the streets, desperate. How can this have happened in just a few days? Why are the images mostly of African Americans? I cannot stay home. I tell Steve I want to go to Texas, to Louisiana, to Mississippi, wherever I can go with the Red Cross to help. He wants to go too, but Steve has not yet taken the required Red Cross training. He calls to volunteer and is told he cannot go without training. The next class may not happen for two weeks. I can't wait—I call and volunteer. This is followed by two days of numerous calls, e-mails, and faxes. Records have to go to Sacramento. I wonder what they are checking. Do they think I'm a registered sex offender, an escaped felon, a parking ticket violator? Why is this taking so long? I've been with the Red Cross for two years, have completed all the classes needed and volunteered on a few local fires. I'm a trained licensed clinical social worker. I have my license, they have my number, what is the problem? Why can't I just go? There must be someone I can help.

The Red Cross has a brand new assistant director. He has been there only one week. I call and pester him every day, along with everyone else I know to pester. A few nights later he calls me at home. It is 8:30 p.m., and he says I can go. I feel as if I have won the lottery.

My vacation time will be used for this trip. Yippee, I don't have to fit into that size two purple dress.

Chapter 2

You Used My Money for What?

Ｏｎ Friday morning, September 2, 2005, I am packed and will leave for the airport in a few hours. Steve is leaving for work. He smiles, but I know something is worrying him. I ask what is wrong. He says he has never learned to do the laundry. We laugh. He practices a load before we leave, adding the soap, and then pushing, pulling, and turning the dials. He writes it all down, step by step, and tapes it on the washer. He leaves for work and I notice all the darks, colors, and whites are humming along together in hot water. His underwear will be pink tonight. Steve is the best thing that has ever happened to me. We have been married for thirty-six years.

I need to go to the ATM a few blocks away to get money for the trip and decide to put on my new Red Cross shirt. It has never been worn, never washed, never shrunk. It has that non-sexy look, somewhere between relaxed and just plain old baggy. It is 6:30 a.m., still early. Laura, my neighbor, is in her driveway. She looks up, sees the red shirt and says with a knowing smile, "I thought you would be going." How did she know? I didn't know myself. I call Baudri, my neighbor next door, and leave a message asking her to look in on Steve because he's not used to my going away and leaving him. Early on in our marriage Steve often went off for business trips to Asia, sometimes for two weeks at a time, and we never thought much about that. We had more of an old-fashioned, traditional relationship than I acknowledged. You Tarzan, go off to hunt; me Jane, stay home, shop, cook, clean. It was actually wonderful at the time.

At the ATM machine outside the bank a man smiles at me. Is he trying to pick me up at 7:00 a.m.? I'm not that beautiful. He waves and says, "I just wrote a check to the Red Cross." I smile back and feel support. We share a commitment and a sense of connection for however fleeting the glance and smile were. This was a beginning of the recognition of how little time and effort it sometimes takes to be inspired and encouraged.

I begin to think about being in devastated areas and wonder what to say to people who may have not eaten for three days. Will they have eaten a meal before we meet? I bring a shopping bag full of cereal bars and tuna packs on the plane. Mental plans are made to buy more snacks upon landing in Houston.

I stop in the office before most people are at work and leave an e-mail to say goodbye to my coworkers, and then realize that fundraising for the Red Cross should not wait until I return. Listening, talking, hugging, and using social work skills feels so insufficient. People need food now. A coworker, Tierney, is in early. I ask if she would be in charge of collecting money for the Red Cross while I am gone.

Tierney is a beautiful young woman with long strawberry-blonde hair. She has a fabulous, natural, fresh-scrubbed, wholesome girl-next-door look. Tierney just went back to school for a new master's degree, works full time, comes in early, and is always involved in advocating for animal rights, the environment, good nutrition, and other good causes. She has a heart of gold. Everyone loves Tierney. She says yes.

A short e-mail is written, saying goodbye to my coworkers. I hand a check to Tierney for $100 to the Red Cross and she begins the drive. We are social workers, counselors, secretaries, fiscal staff, managers, and similar professions. It is a nonprofit agency. No one earns a huge salary, and I expect Tierney will collect a few hundred dollars.

Steve meets me at work and we drive to the airport. It feels strange. Steve always handles the tickets, hotel reservations, and rental cars, and I let him. He always takes care of me. We say goodbye, not knowing if cell phones will work, electricity will be on, or where I will be. It is good that he will have a busy week—he won't have time to worry.

Inside the gate at the airport, while standing in line for tickets, there are two young men who smile at me. Mike and George are just eighteen years old. In a few weeks George will go into the Marine Corps, and he says he will be in Iraq. They both see my red shirt and excitedly say, "Hey, we are Red Cross too." A bond begins. They show a caring nature when I briefly misplace my boarding pass (it was in my back pocket instead of my folder). Mike offers to carry my bag, and goes back to the gate to check for my pass. I feel embarrassed that the pass seems lost. They are new and I'm setting a terrible example by being disorganized before even getting out of the gate. They are going to be great Red Crossers. They take charge, are compassionate, and I feel cared for even though we met only a few moments ago.

We board the plane and end up sitting far apart. An hour passes and I find some forms Mike and George will need to know how to fill out. I get out of my seat and walk down the aisle to the front of the plane where Mike and George are sitting. A pretty young woman behind me is named Maggie. She sees the red shirt, taps me on the shoulder and says, "Hey, I'm Red Cross too." She is smart, well-organized, and knows how to take charge. She points across the aisle to a young woman sitting on the other side. Alisha, she tells me, is from Chicago and she is Red Cross too. They both work for Cisco. I expect they are both light years ahead of me on technology. After all, they both work in a very prestigious, high-tech company in one of the most competitive, progressive areas in the nation, and probably the world. I try not to badger myself for thinking I'm less technically adept and decide to focus on how great it is that these bright, young, enthusiastic Silicon Valley minds have joined us.

Just before landing Maggie speaks to an airline steward and asks that he make an announcement to find out how many people on the plane are with the Red Cross. He makes the announcement and ten hands go up. Maggie asks the steward to suggest that we all meet at the baggage claim around the woman in the red shirt. We will organize and strategize about where we are going. The steward makes the announcement, and then adds a thank-you to us for going. The whole plane erupts in spontaneous applause. Wearing red is certainly a good beginning.

After landing at the Houston airport we all meet in the terminal, call headquarters, and are told to go to a hotel at the airport for the night. I was prepared for a shelter, but it was late evening and we have to be at an early morning briefing at the airport. We are therefore assigned to a hotel at the airport to expedite arrival for the early morning briefing. We arrive at the hotel and the reservations clerk greets us cheerily. She tells us to find a partner, sign a sheet of paper with our names, and she will give us a key. Wow, how do they know who we are? Anyone can ask for a room.

I marvel at how they have cut through the red tape and simplified paperwork. IDs are not even taken. I make a mental note to harass my supervisor when I get back home about the need to eliminate paperwork and unnecessary details, and focus on what is really important. This has long been an ongoing issue for me, and here today it all seems so clear. Why do we get bogged down with multiple reports and multiple ways of saying the same thing? When looking for a new job, my work history of thirty years got put on a one-page resume . . . why is this so hard to understand?

We start to pick partners to share a room with, and I choose a tall, good-looking young man who is one-third my age. It breaks the ice, and we all laugh. Steve, if you are reading this, I really shared a room with Alisha, the smart young woman from Chicago.

We get to the room and I'm amazed. I call Steve to say we arrived safely, proceed to tell him the name of the great hotel where we are staying, and indicate the thread count of the sheets. "*Is that what you used my money for?*" he yells. "Tell the Red Cross to buy food and clothing for people." He is mad and definitely a bit jealous that I'm having a good time while he is at home, lonely, and trying to defrost a frozen dinner.

Chapter 3

The Briefing

IT IS SATURDAY morning, September 3, 2005. I decide to skip breakfast and work out in the hotel exercise room, thinking this will be the last luxury for the next ten days. The weather will be hot and humid, and if I don't work out I will not have the stamina to keep up. There are so many young, trim, healthy-looking twenty-somethings around me, and it would feel awful not to be able to keep up with them. Alisha is half my age. She is athletic and very energetic. She goes for breakfast. Life does not seem fair. How does she get to look so great and not have to work out this morning? I hope there will be something to eat at the briefing.

We leave the hotel at the Houston airport at 7:30 a.m. and board a shuttle to another hotel for meetings and assignments. There are several busloads of us. We are men and women, young and old. We are mostly Caucasian. We chat on the short ride. I introduce myself to a young man behind me. He is in his late twenties or early thirties. He has a short, blond, military, crew-cut-type haircut and huge, powerful arms. He is an ex-marine, a firefighter, and a paramedic. He is the one who climbs down the ropes when helicopters pull people to safety. He has done this in the last war and is highly experienced. He volunteered for 9-11 in New York a few years ago. I'm mesmerized. I'm a social worker, I know how to talk.

He talks about how he gave mouth-to-mouth resuscitation to a seven-year-old boy, only to have the child die in his arms. He has young children at home and said he could not help but think about them. I ask him how he got through that. "You suck it up," he says. I ask him if he ever talks about that with other guys. "No, we don't talk about that," he says. He sounds so strong. I worry about the toll of not expressing these thoughts and feelings, and the consequences of suppressing them over the years.

We arrive at a large hotel near the airport. About 150 people are at the hotel for the first briefing. We are ushered downstairs to a huge room. It is the kind of room that hotels reserve for conventions, weddings, and bar mitzvahs. It is boringly beige and has pullout partitions, the kind used to open or close off parts of the room in order to accommodate different-sized events. Kind of a not-one-size fits all. We mill around in lines, signing sheets at different tables, and are told we will get assignments after the briefing. A box of glazed donuts sits on a table at the entrance. I ignore it, thinking this meeting will be over soon, and maybe the local Red Cross chapter will bring us something healthy, such as fruit or yogurt. This is my first big mistake, expecting someone will take care of me. It is reminiscent of childhood. Me daddy, pay bills, take care of you child. After an hour the soggy-looking glazed donuts begin to have a magnetic force and I succumb. An hour later it happens again. They are not even good but I eat them out of anxiety. These old ineffective ways of coping with anxiety emerge. Where will I go, who will be with me, what will I say. We are all still strangers.

We are summoned to the center of the room for an official Red Cross meeting. Two people are at the front, ready to speak. The first is a Caucasian woman who seems to be in her forties. She appears conservative with a short, very practical hairstyle. She sounds as if she has done this for years and conveys an aura of experience. She gives a general thanks and pep talk for coming. It is upbeat. While it is a welcomed speech there is not much that was unexpected and it is not gripping or overly inspirational. As I peruse the room it is clear that we, the volunteers, are overwhelmingly Caucasian. She tells us we will be in teams of three and will drive to different locations throughout the state to work in shelters. She tells us she has just come from working in a shelter and had an infant throw up on her. She begins to talk about what to expect.

The young man speaks next. He is young, probably in his very early twenties. His hair is loose, very curly. He looks as if he has long lived in the community and knows the people. In California it is politically correct to say African American. His words are the most memorable. He tells us that the population we will work with is mostly poor and black. He is black and uses the word black. "Many may not have had a shower," he says. He reminds us that many have been "plucked from roofs" of their homes, from boats, and from the water. "If you cannot be near someone who smells, go home! If you cannot be near someone who may have worn the same clothes for days, go home! If you cannot hug a black person go home! The people need to be touched, held, and hugged."

In his calm and direct way he has shared the importance of physical contact. He goes on to tell us this is a religious part of the country. There is a strong presence of churches. People may want to pray. He advises us to put aside our own values and get down on our knees with people to pray if it will comfort them. I think about my own religion and decide he is right. We are here to comfort and to bring a message of hope. I think about my wonderful Rabbi Magat back home in San Jose, and I know he would agree. He would want me to join and connect. Don't worry, Reb; I'm not converting, just praying.

The briefing room is large; we mill about. Most of us are still relative strangers. We wait for our names to be called to know which group we will be in and where we will be deployed. I look at the donuts again and remember I packed cereal bars. I eat a cereal bar even though I'm not really hungry. Most people will be called within two hours or so. I wonder what I can do with this time. Then I connect with a wonderful, athletic, good-looking young man named David. He is lean and muscular. He definitely works out. He appears to be in his mid-twenties. Later I will learn he is forty. Wow! How many crunches must it take to look like that? Could I ever bench press more than five pounds? I have to remember to keep exercising on this trip. It is just one more way to torture myself with thoughts of still more things to do on this trip. It is one more way to try to measure up. Measure up to what? I consciously know the futility of this venture. I consciously know I will never be ninety-two pounds of muscular, sensual, swimsuit-edition material for the front cover of *Sports Illustrated* . . . so why do I keep trying? How much world approval and recognition do I need? Ah, I have to admit the media still has a hold on me to look like some unachievable, unrealistic goddess.

David works at Cisco. He reminds me of my son, David, who is also an excellent and patient teacher. Both my David and this David have great social skills. People want to be with them. He puts me at ease about my lack of knowledge. I do not feel stupid, only inexperienced. David is very knowledgeable about technology. What else would I expect? He works at Cisco. I'm a techno klutz. I'm embarrassed to say I still don't know all the functions on my cell phone, which I have had for a year. We talk. David patiently teaches me how to text message. I have no use for this potentially earthshaking and life-changing skill other than to impress my own twenty-nine-year-old son. It will let my son think I can function in the current world.

David is personable and lets me hold the phone to push the buttons while he tells me what to do. He is an excellent teacher and knows the best way to learn is for hands-on experience. He doesn't have to physically hold the phone. He doesn't have to be in such control. He knows that he knows what he needs to know. He doesn't ask me to repeat back;

there are no quizzes. He is confident. David's name is now called and he goes to join a group for another briefing. The next and last time I will see him will be out of the corner of my eye in a shelter where I will sleep in Baton Rouge that night at about eleven o'clock. I will be tired and trying to sleep.

It will be five hours of sitting around before I will find out where I will be deployed. I decide to use this time to mill around and make small talk. Everyone seems calm, some people are reading, and some are lying down on the floor with their heads on backpacks. Some are trying to catch up on sleep. I decide my job here as a mental health professional should not wait until I get an assignment. I decide it should start here with the staff. I carefully note the tenor of the room with the volunteers. No one seems to need me.

Again and again I scan the room, trying to use my best social work skills to pick up the slightest unrest. Aha! Across the room is the strong ex-marine with whom I rode on the bus. He is now looking upset. He is searching the luggage area, checking his bag, looking for something. His cell phone is missing. He checks all around the room, checks his pockets, and has the Houston Red Cross staff make an announcement several times. No one finds his phone. He leaves the room and is gone for twenty minutes. When he returns he looks still more distraught. He has been to the lobby of the hotel to check the registration desk, and has been to the lost and found. The phone has not been turned in. I go along with him to search the room together two or three times more.

He is sure the phone was near his bag and is now sure someone has taken it. As time passes he becomes more and more angry. How could someone do this? We are all volunteers in this room and have come to help. He has young children at home and a young wife who is ill. "I just want to go home," he says. He may not stay. This phone was his link to home. I go to talk with the staff about this and they tell me he can call home from the desk phone. When I tell him this, it does not seem to calm him. He just bought a new phone and paid several hundred dollars for a calling card. It was a huge investment for him, and now someone has picked it up and can use it. He remains angry

He goes outside to the front of the hotel and paces about. I follow to be with him and talk. He seems mildly irritated. I tell him if he wants me to bug off to say so. He is more polite and says he would like to be alone. Twenty minutes later he returns to the main room and lies down on the floor with his head on his luggage. I lie down on the floor next to him and talk. "What is the worst of it?" I ask. Here again is a learning experience for me and that is not to assume I know the answer without asking. I think he will say that the worst of it is that he cannot be in contact with his family. Instead he says it is that someone would steal from him. Though this is intriguing to me as a social worker, and I would love to delve into this, our timeframes and the setting do not allow for much processing, or for long conversations about loss. Instead, we talk about the possibility of getting a new phone. He could get a new one for only $30. I would have offered to give him the money if that were really the issue. We talk about the calling card that someone else can use. He just loaded the phone with about $400 worth of minutes. I ask if it can be cancelled. He says no, that can't be done. Again, he tells me he wants to leave to go home.

My first thinking is to talk with him about taking care of himself and going home if he needs to do so. Instead, I ask him to tell me more about how he has managed crisis in the past. "What kinds of tough things have you faced in the past?" I ask. He briefly talks about wartime, seeing buddies wounded and killed, the child he tried to revive on 9-11 who still died in his arms.

"So you have seen and faced death before and gotten through it?" I say. "The worst of this time is that you are out about $600. On a scale of one to ten, where would you put this loss of $600 compared to past losses? You told me you faced all these life-threatening challenges in life, have come through these, and now you say you can't deal with this one?" I think of a seminar I once took with David Burns, a noted Stanford professor and psychiatrist who is a prominent author and well-respected in the field of psychology. He is a superstar in the field of cognitive approaches. I hope he would be proud of this line of questioning. At this point this furious ex-marine turns to me and smiles. "Are you a pastor?" he asks.

Sometime later in the day he returns again and says he was able to stop the card from being used and will not be losing that money. He still does not have the phone. The next day I see him in Baton Rouge. It will be the last time we see each other, and he has stayed. I hug him and say I'm glad he stayed. We need his skill. I wonder where he will be assigned. Will he go down in baskets to pull children, parents, and grandparents off roofs?

The five hours of waiting during orientation has not been a waste. I hope I have made some difference today. I would like to think I had some influence on his decision to stay. We have kept a valuable volunteer with us, and I like to think somehow I had a part in his decision-making process. At any rate I really love the hugging part. It seems so easy and so welcomed.

It has been about three hours of waiting in the briefing room. By now most of the volunteers in the room have been assigned to a location and are gone. I wonder if the national staff has forgotten me. Did I forget to fill in a blank somewhere? Did they decide I don't know enough about DSM diagnosis to qualify as a real licensed clinical social worker? Do I know the difference between an adjustment disorder and paranoid schizophrenia? I amuse myself with such thoughts and go back to all the self-doubts of my past. It does not last long. They say I'm still on the list and they are working on it.

The second wave of volunteers has come through and there is a new briefing. I've heard it before but decide to listen again. When it is time for questions one of the volunteers, an older man, asks how high his snake boots should be. Wait a minute, what was that question? What are snake boots? He pulls up one pant leg to reveal boots reaching about nine inches up his ankle and asks if these are high enough. One of the volunteers goes over to the older volunteer's leg, places his hand about twelve inches from the ground, and says the snakes usually bite "right about here." There are comedians in every group. Clearly this is three inches or more higher than his boots cover. I take this all seriously and think, I did not sign on for this. People, yes; water moccasins, mosquitoes, alligators, no! There is nothing I signed that prepared me for this. It is the first time I think seriously about passing out and going home. My head is dizzy, and it is not just from insufficient water or food. I literally lie down on the floor so as not to fall down.

The room is almost empty, and again I annoy those in charge to be sure my name is on the list. It has been five hours of sitting in this briefing room. The staff is growing testy with me, and I am becoming impatient. I am to learn that this is the modus operandi. It is called organized chaos. For anyone used to moving quickly, either efficiently or inefficiently, for anyone who can't wait to get things done, for anyone who hates bumbling, this place would be death. I think about Steve. He has his own business, belongs to several organizations, and has a hard time doing "nothing." Maybe he would not have been happy here. I think about all the management teams at my own job back home with the continual penchant for perfect paperwork, with the numerous, ongoing checklists for knowing what the status of work is, with the illusion that work is under control. They would hate it here.

I am to learn this will happen over and over and over again during the time here. Yes, it feels chaotic. That is the point. We are in chaos, we are in crisis, and the staff is doing their best. This is overwhelming and one does not have a comforting sense of control. This creates anxiety and who wants to live with that? Just ask me. At the very least, today I am diagnosable as Axis I, Clinical Disorder 293.02, Generalized Anxiety Disorder NOS . . . what will it be tomorrow?

Chapter 4

I'd Rather Die

THERE ARE LARGE, handwritten signs that have been taped with masking tape to the wall. They are lists of things to buy if we did not bring them with us. Sleeping mats, bug spray with DEET, and so on. We are told to use sprays since the mosquitoes are big, vicious, and ugly. I wonder if the mosquitoes think we are big, vicious, and ugly.

Other things listed are latex gloves, snacks, and a bathing suit. Bathing suit? Are we off to Hawaii? What is a bathing suit for? I'm told we may not have private showers; hence the need for bathing suits. Does that mean we will shower with men? I'm in denial about the lack of comfort we may encounter. I have never slept in a shelter, and wonder what it will be like. At home I'm used to privacy. What will it be like to use a small bathroom with fifty other women who are all in a rush to get out at the same time? I stay in denial. Will we remain polite with each other, or will the stress of time and long hours begin to affect us too? What will it be like to not sleep a full eight hours? At home I'm a grump if Steve wakes me early or wants to talk in the middle of the night. I put this out of my head and think, I'm a social worker and can make peace if anyone gets upset. We will all be rational and talk about things such as how we are all in this together, sort of a rah-rah, we-all-need-to-be-a-team thing.

They call this a hardship assignment and we are told there will be extra money put on our preloaded debit cards to spend for the extra things we did not pack and may need. Oh great, so now, instead of being relieved by not having to fit into a dress, I have to fit into a bathing suit, and worse yet may have to wear it in front of strange men . . . and be compared with all those trim and fit twenty-year-olds. Maybe this idea was not so great after all.

Finally, my name is called. I am on a team with two other women. We will all be in groups of three. Each group will be assigned to different locations in Texas and Louisiana. Both women on my team are from the South, they have some maturity and life experience and are in their thirties or early forties. We are assigned to work in Baton Rouge in Louisiana. We are told to go to the Houston airport to rent a car and then drive to the Red Cross chapter in Baton Rouge. One woman is super-organized. She agrees to be the one to rent the car and take the first shift of driving. She is clearly used to taking charge, and I am happy to sit in the backseat. It will take us seven to eight hours to get there with the stops for gas, shopping, eating, and getting lost.

Before we leave for Houston we find the directions taped on the wall for how to get to a local Walgreen's and Wal-Mart on the way to our assignments. There will be precious little time to shop. We are told Wal-Mart will have the supplies we need and that they have been restocking for this disaster. After we get our cars at the airport, we are to spend fifteen to thirty minutes shopping so that we can quickly get back to our cars and drive to our assignments. I think about Sandy, my fabulous coworker back at home. She will kill me for shopping at Wal-Mart. She is very concerned about fair labor practices and fair pay for workers. Sandy is bright and politically astute, and I've listened to her in awe. Then I hear that Wal-Mart has just donated $17 to $19 million to this effort. I rationalize that it is okay to shop there. There really is no time now for a controversy or a political dialogue about allegations of poor wages, sex discrimination, international horrendous child labor practices, forced closure of small community business due to unfair tax advantages, pollution, and all the other stories that have surfaced about Wal-Mart. Even if I knew the fine points of these accusations, with dates, names, and places, there simply are no other places to shop now (that being one of the points of the argument re: unfair competition). This ethical battle will have to wait for another time of life. I hope Sandy will understand and that she will still be my friend.

We strategize and decide to not go to the closest Wal-Mart because we expect that everyone else from this Red Cross chapter office will be there. We want to be sure they are not sold out of sleeping mats, and we need to make time because we won't get to Baton Rouge until dark. We will have a better chance of finding things at a different location. We are assured by everyone in town that there are many Wal-Marts along the way from Houston to the Louisiana border on route 10. They are right. There are several, and we find one an hour away near the border of Louisiana. We plan what we need, split up, and agree to spend no more than fifteen to thirty minutes to be out the door and back to the car.

We pick up sleeping mats, pillows, latex gloves, and disinfectant; I buy several more boxes of cereal bars. We look for bathing suits. There is a large sign, BATHING SUITS $3. I think, Wow, how great, they know we all need them and have gone out of their way to accommodate us. I'm so excited. There are two round double-tiered racks filled with suits. There are numerous choices—bright, colorful suits in yellows, purples, greens. Some have stripes, flowers, and polka dots. There is one problem, however: none of them have more than five square inches of fabric. They are all teeny-weeny bikinis. I don't mind being open and honest with emotions, but I'm not yet liberated enough to let all the wrinkles and cellulite be out for public viewing. I'd rather be dead!

I decide against these suits and quickly find a more modest-looking, boring gray jogging top and shorts that I can wear in a shower. We pay for everything at one of those do-it-yourself scanning counters. I'm so proud of myself for having learned to use these back home. It helps us get through the line more quickly. I only get stumped once and need help to scan the nectarines, which don't have bar codes. I bought them to share on the trip. This is my attempt to choose wholesome food. It is also my insecurity as I contemplate that it might be nine days more till we see any fruit.

When I was a child and my family took a trip almost anywhere we always packed food. My aunts would pack food for us to take home after Passover and Thanksgiving dinners. We would get tinfoil packages of turkey and other leftovers. Today, whenever Steve and I take trips, I still pack food. At the end of any meal when my son, David, has come over for dinner I offer to pack food for him to take home with him. He only lives twenty minutes away. He gets miffed with me, tries to hide his dismay while demonstrating some eye rolling, and sometimes he placates me by taking a peach.

This packing of food is reminiscent of my heritage. My parents and grandparents escaped persecution and poverty in Poland about eighty years ago. This time, here in the South, will remind me many times over of the stories about the near-starvation of my mother. She kept a crust of bread under her pillow to nibble at for the days when she was without food as a young child back in Poland during the rise of the Nazis. She was the lucky one. She got the bread because she was the baby. Though I was born in this country and never experienced starvation, the fear and sadness has permeated through to my life from the generations before. The sadness has never gone away. The fear remains. I'm always planning the next meal. It is partly why I have always been overweight. I'm always carrying that extra food on my body; it creates the illusion of security. I have food on me just in case I get kidnapped, separated from the nearest supermarket, or in this case face the reality of a disaster. The experiences with Katrina will touch that heritage many times during these ten days.

We drive another hour or so and stop at a local fast food place. The staff members who are behind the counter are now talking about danger in the nearby towns. There is one story of people losing property and guarding their homes with guns. We are not sure if it is rumor but we decide that we need to get moving to be in Baton Rouge before night. It is surreal. My sheltered life has never put me in a neighborhood of violence with guns or knives. I have been lucky. I do not consciously believe the danger is real or that it is only a few miles away. This is called denial. One of the women in our group has wisely taken the cell phone number of one of the Red Cross men volunteers. He is in a car on the same road ahead of us in case we need help. What he could do in a dangerous situation is beyond me, but we still like the protective image that men project. I am glad she has done this.

On the way we see caravans of huge sixteen-wheeler trucks heading toward Baton Rouge. They have large pieces of paper taped to the back of the trucks. The signs say: **Disaster Supplies for Hurricane Katrina Victims.** I am impressed with how many trucks are headed there, and I want to pull up beside them to honk and give them a thumbs-up sign. We do so and see huge company logos on the sides of the trucks. The signage indicates the trucks are those of a national beer company. We laugh and hope they are bringing other needed supplies.

We arrive in Baton Rouge and call to find out which shelter we will be sleeping in. We are given the name of a Methodist church and an address. We ask five different local townspeople to direct us. We get lost over and over again. One man even offers to drive us to the church. We follow him and it is the wrong church. Everyone wants to be helpful. It is night and it is dark. No one in town says they don't know where the church is. The local residents all give us different directions. I wonder if this is a cultural thing—that people all want to help and can't admit they don't know how to tell us to get there. I wonder if we are all so tired we can't follow directions.

We are tired and getting grumpy. We decide to find a police department. That too is hard to find. Finally we find one. A young police officer gives us a police escort and I feel special. He stays with us for awhile and we unload our bags at the church, which serves as a shelter. He tells us that the town had about 200,000 people two weeks ago and today there are about 400,000. Before we leave in the next few days it will be close to 500,000. There has to be an enormous strain on the police, but he smiles. Though he has been working long hours he is polite and helpful. He seems to want to stay with us, and he hangs out in the parking lot. Over and over again we are to be surrounded by people wanting to bond. It is powerful and wonderful. Disaster has brought out the best in so many people here in the South. I begin to feel a kinship with people who will sometimes connect for only minutes, yet the power and support that is conveyed cannot be dismissed.

We are volunteers and new to the town and yet there is a wonderful, immediate sense of camaraderie with this young police officer. I expect it is probably like this in the armed services when a disaster calls for immediate cooperation. Working together for a cause can bring out the best in total strangers, and we will see this again and again during this time in Louisiana. It was this kind of experience that was so uplifting and inspiring.

We go into the church. Inside, we find cots, say a few hellos, and exhaustedly get ready to sleep. I have never slept in a shelter and so I decide to keep my money and ID under the pillow. The old former New York upbringing puts me into immediate autopilot response. This response to guard everything was internalized early, growing up in crowded areas in New York.

I have put on a T-shirt and jogging shorts to sleep in. No one told me what the well-dressed Red Cross volunteer wears to such functions, but I found that some women wear shorts, some wear pajamas, some wear jogging pants. Some men wear only their pants and no tops. It is warm and sticky. It is humid. I have thoughts of a wanting to remove my T-shirt and sleep in comfort. Tonight I'm envious of men. I decide this is not the place to practice my liberal thoughts about sleeping attire. I keep my shirt on.

As I attempt to relax enough to sleep, I make a mental note to suggest that the Red Cross design and sell long red jersey nightgowns with white crosses on them. They could be great items. Could they sell for Christmas? I'm wishing I had one now. There could be pajamas for men and women. These would be lightweight, easy to pack and wash. Maybe I will become a fashion designer when I get back.

It feels like there are several hundred of us sleeping in cots on the floor. I don't know the actual number but estimate that we probably number about 150 to 200. We are men and women, old and young, primarily Caucasian and some African American, Asian, and Hispanic. We sleep in one huge, open room. This is used for church functions during the year. A flashlight is placed under my cot, and then the bathroom is checked out, knowing I will be getting up during the night. In the middle of the night more people come in. That is where I see David for the last time. He is helping with a new delivery of cots. It is late, about eleven thirty or so, and he is still energetic. Although it is not his job, David is helping bring cots into a shelter where we are to spend the night. He is clearly a joiner, a team player, and a leader. I can barely keep my eyelids up. I make another mental note to find time to exercise in the morning. Late in the night a young man tries to find his way to his cot near mine. It is dark. I direct him to his cot using my flashlight on the floor. If my real day job does not work out I can always use this experience in a resume and apply to be an usher in a theater.

I sleep no more than three hours, at most. My anxiety was beginning to take hold again and I wake at five or so in the morning. After doing some crunches on the floor and thinking about going out to jog, I decide it would be better not to chance the unknown neighborhood or the mosquitoes. Instead, I just run in place in a corner in the dark for twenty minutes. Some other early risers pass by and give me a smile. I am the only one doing this. Am I totally nuts?

It is important to be in the bathroom early so as not to have to jockey for position with fifty or more women. One woman with gray hair is carefully applying eyeliner, and is using a hairdryer and a curling iron. I try not to be judgmental, but it is hard. I have barely enough energy to brush my teeth and remember deodorant. More than pulling my hair back with a rubber band is not on my list of things to do today. I dress early, pack my sheets and towels, and am ready to leave for headquarters. It is 6:45 or 7:00 a.m.

Almost everyone is out of bed and in various states of dress. At this time one man storms rapidly down the middle of the aisle and stops right in front of me. In a very loud voice, and with tremendous, wildly expressive energy, he begins to sing:

> *Oh, what a beautiful mornin', oh, what a beautiful day.*
> *I got a beautiful feelin' ev'rything's goin' my way.*

These are of course some lines from the well-known song from *Oklahoma!* It is early morning and the demeanor and expectation of the room is for dignified, respectful, and simple quiet time. We are respecting each other's space as we simply try to finish dressing, determine if there will be breakfast, and figure out where we are going. The singing man continues to come near me. Who is he? Everyone is stunned, and the place is suddenly totally silent. I think he must be diagnosable. What to do? I decide to give him a hug. Everyone in the room, all one hundred or more volunteers, break out in applause. He walks out the door. He is a volunteer, and now everyone realizes this was his way to start the morning on a high note. This is how the experience goes. All the normal, quiet routines we generally find at work, in life, seem to be suspended for this occasion. What might generally be considered a little bit over the edge, a little bit nutty, is tolerated, encouraged, and embraced. At least that is how this day begins.

We quickly leave for headquarters and try hard not to get lost again. We are slightly more successful this time.

Chapter 5

When Do I Start?

TODAY IS SUNDAY, September 4. Finally, we are in Baton Rouge at chapter headquarters where I hook up with my unit in mental health. At last I can use my skills and feel productive. We have a wonderful supervisor, Judy. She is warm, organized, and knowledgeable. There are about a dozen of us at this mental health briefing. Judy will decide where we are to go and whom we will work with. We will work in teams of two. I am happy to know this since it is my first time on a national disaster and it will be good to be with someone who is more experienced. We turn in our names again. Now we need to show proof of current licensing, and the staff copies all this down. There are a few minor crises to attend to while we are getting to know each other, and Judy assigns people to handle each one. She asks me to do a debriefing for a volunteer who has to leave immediately. Aha, I have finally started. I can actually use a skill I have been trained in.

I talk with a man who has to leave to catch a plane back home to California in about an hour. He is an older man in his sixties or seventies, and I relate to him easily. He has to leave because his wife is seriously ill back home, and his health has not allowed him to tolerate the heat here. He feels like a failure because he has only been here a few days and is not able to complete the assignment. Leaving before finishing an assignment can be considered a failure by volunteers. The choice to leave is of course the right one for him and he has made it himself. He understands the philosophy of having to take care of yourself first before you are able to care for someone else. He has only a few more minutes and has to catch his ride to the airport. We don't have time for a full debriefing. I ask him if this is his first time volunteering. "Oh no," he says, "this is my sixteenth time!" I hug him and cannot understand how he considers this is a failure. He has done the right thing. I want him to feel good about his efforts, but we have no more time to talk. This is not a good beginning. I don't feel complete.

I return to my group, and we continue getting to know each other. A volunteer hurriedly comes to us and says she needs a mental health worker to work with a family that has just arrived outside. They are blocking her car. She has to leave, and she cannot back her car out. She is annoyed.

I will get another chance. Judy asks me to go out. I go out and say hello to the family, which consists of a husband, wife, grandmother, and several teenage and young children. They have just driven up in their car from a flooded area in New Orleans to find the Red Cross. They do not have a place to stay, and are looking for shelter. The grandmother has diabetes and does not have any medication. They are all in the hot sun. My big professional success here is getting them to move their car. This calms the other volunteer. All these years of studying for a license have finally paid off. It has not been in vain as I deftly spot some chairs where they can sit under a tree and suggest they move their car to a more comfortable place in the shade. After telling them I am not familiar with this area in Baton Rouge, that I am from out of state, and bringing bottles of water, I inform them I will go inside to find some answers and will return in a few minutes. In the meantime my new supervisor, Judy, helps find a nurse to go out to assess the grandmother. The chapter does not store medications on site. The family will have to go somewhere else for medical care, and then we will find a shelter.

A nurse goes out to talk with the family and I go inside to try to find a shelter for the family. All the volunteers inside seem to be from California. None of them knows this area. I hear there are 800 volunteers from California and feel great pride. This pride is not helpful in finding a shelter for the family. The list of available shelters is still forming. We do not yet know which have bathrooms or showers, who can take the disabled, and so forth. After finding some possibilities, and then going back out to find the family, they cannot be found. They are gone. I assume and hope that the nurse was able to direct them for medical care to a local hospital, and I hope that is where they have gone. The shelter will wait.

After returning to my group I am paired up with a wonderful, experienced, sensitive social worker from Northern California. Her name is Sue. We will be a team for the rest of the time. We drive to the Baton Rouge airport, rent a car, and return to get our first assignment. It is to assess shelters. I am upset. I did not come all the way out here to look at buildings. However, that is what is needed right now, and I learn to do what is needed. (Hmm, I wonder if I should sign up for the army.) Without this information we don't know where to send people who need shelters. Sue and I go out to visit two churches. One houses about 500 to 600 people. They are doing an excellent job.

The congregation has donated food and clothing, and it is a beautiful, bright, clean facility. We talk with the shelter manager and I jokingly suggest she should get a five-star rating in the AAA Guide Book for motorists. She laughs in a good-natured way. Next, we talk with the single social worker running the mental health unit for all 600 residents and we provide support for her. She has been overwhelmed with need, has no other mental health staff to support her, and although she is doing a superb job she was beginning to have some self-doubts. She soon was validated with our support. In a rush to provide aid to those who experienced this disaster it is too easy to overlook the need to support our own volunteers. If they are not cared for they cannot do this tremendous job. Although eager to meet and work with those who survived this hurricane, I also began to wish we had time to visit all thirty-three, or fifty, or however many churches there were on the list who work with the mental health staffs, pastors, police, and whoever else was volunteering too.

Next we go to a small church and meet with their pastor. He and his congregation are also doing a fabulous job. He is sad that he has to close the shelter tomorrow because they have religious school starting and will no longer have room for a shelter. A large family pulls up in a van asking where they can get food. The pastor has food that he provides for the family. We ask the family if they have a place to stay, and in an attempt to bond with them we share the information that Sue and I still don't know where we will be staying either. The young black husband says they will all be staying with a relative here in Baton Rouge and quickly, unhesitatingly, says Sue and I can stay with them. It is so incredibly touching that this man who clearly has a large family he is trying to provide for, with so many unknowns in front of him, offers to care for two more strangers of a different culture, race, and age. Once again it is clear how the very best intent and actions can be seen and felt during this disaster in so many people.

The pastor tells of how he was getting ready to go home at ten o'clock one night after a very long day when a bus with forty-five people pulled up seeking shelter. He returned to set up cots and prepare a place for them. A twelve-year-old in the congregation had been especially helpful and was now inspired to become a pastor. The wonderful thing to consider is how far-reaching these efforts will be for years to come. Here was a youngster whose future may develop based on seeing the meaningful efforts of his pastor. He made a huge impact on the lives of others, and it is so marvelous to be able to see and feel this by being able to be here in person. Again, the experience of being here is so powerful, and it never could be the same through making financial contributions alone. It is such great fortune to be able to be here physically and work alongside the people involved in this community.

Chapter 6

Are We There Yet?

ON SUNDAY NIGHT Sue and I are assigned to sleep in a second shelter in Baton Rouge. It is a wonderful Baptist church. Of course we get lost again as we have so many times before, but that is getting to be part of the package. I want to get a good Thomas Guide map and cannot find one for Louisiana. It is past six o'clock and most stores are closed. We find a Walgreen's drugstore and they have a Thomas Guide for Baton Rouge. It is about twenty dollars, but that is just for the city of Baton Rouge. We may be assigned to another city in the morning, and therefore decide to wait till morning. Getting lost has taken its toll. We have spent many hours on this trip getting lost and it is beginning to wear at my normally outwardly pleasant manner. If we go many more days like this I will not be so patient.

We finally find the church we are assigned to, and it is such a treat. After signing in I am met by three men who follow me out to the car to carry my things. One takes a bag, one takes a sleeping mat, and one carries my towel. The Ritz Carlton could not have provided better service. True, it is early and the shelter is not full yet, but this is unbelievable. I have never experienced so much attentiveness.

One of the church women provides a tour. The bathroom has freshly washed towels that the church families have provided. There is a wonderful assortment of soaps, shampoos, packages of DEET for mosquitoes, and all kinds of other toiletries. She gives a tour of the kitchen and is so proud of the food that has been provided for us. Fresh fruit, two kinds of milk (two-percent and whole), cereals, peanut butter, jelly, and white bread. I have two pieces of bread with peanut butter for dinner this evening, and they are delicious. They are reminiscent of childhood: soft, soothing textures and familiar food. They are comforting tonight, and I decide that not every single meal has to have green vegetables and beta carotene included.

During the night one of the men who is a church member sits at a table reading a book throughout the night to keep watch. It is an incredible experience for me. The people in this parish are so giving and expressive of their appreciation for our willingness to come to Louisiana to help. It is clear that the churches have held these neighborhoods together. They have provided the care and comfort needed in this time. There is no way the Red Cross, FEMA, or other agencies could possibly have acted so quickly and held this together without the support of the churches. This observation will leave lasting impressions about the importance of the churches' neighbors, families, and community bonds for the rest of my life. We were to see this over and over again with the vast number of churches assuming such a great part of the responsibility of helping the victims of the disaster.

We rise early and go back to the Red Cross headquarters. During the night local Red Cross chapter headquarters has moved to a new location in a new building. Though this must have been planned for a long time, there could not be a worse time to have a major move, but that is what happened. The entire headquarters moved during the night to a new facility. It is much larger, but the added logistics of pulling phone lines, setting up computers, tables, chairs, records, food, water, a post office, and so forth, must have required a Herculean effort, accompanied by many bottles of Tylenol. Of course we get lost again.

Sue and I were assigned to visit shelters to evaluate them for the kinds of services they were able to provide, and we assumed we were to assess how well they were doing. The list of shelters we were given to tour must have numbered over fifty. Though we were not expected to see all of them, we began to see the value in visiting these centers, we were also greatly relieved at no longer being assigned to assess any more shelters. We are finally given an assignment to work in a shelter in Monroe, north of Baton Rouge.

Now we are free to drive to our assignment. It is about four to five hours' drive north, depending on how lost we will get. We do not know anything about the town of Monroe and though we are eager to be on our way, we also want to take time to find some toys to take with us for the children. We stop at a large discount store to buy crayons, coloring books, balloons, and other toys to take with us to the shelter. It is disappointing because they have such a poor selection of small toys. We buy a few bags of balloons and then head out for another store. Time is at a premium and we cannot scour the town looking for the perfect store.

More and more I want to capture some of the images of this event on film. Of course I have no idea at this time how momentous this time in history will eventually prove to be. Back in California at the Red Cross I was advised not to bring a camera or cell phone because of the high probability of theft. "Who will watch these things while you take a shower?" one Red Cross staff member back home asked. At that time, while still back home, the fear of losing a possession got to me and I did not take a camera. Fortunately, this same advice was not listened to about a cell phone. We could barely have survived without one. That was the single worst piece of advice given before we left home.

No one should come on a national disaster without a cell phone. We were often on the road in small towns, often late at night. It could be a total nightmare and a danger to be without a cell phone. It would be foolhardy not to protect ourselves with one. Almost everyone has a cell phone. Better to take the risk of losing a possession than not be safe.

So I have no camera, and more and more I know I will want to have these images when I get back home. There are such powerful moments, both personally and historically, and photos for me are one of the best ways to keep them in my memory. I decide to buy a camera, but I know nothing about cameras. Should it be a disposable one, and then it won't matter if it gets lost? Not having packed a copy of *Consumer's Reports*, means having to depend on the best advice of a salesperson. Wal-Mart does not stand out in my mind for excellence with respect to customer service. It is not equated in my mind with a staff which has been given the luxury of lots of free time to develop product knowledge and an incentive to serve customers well. They have become a low-price leader for a reason. It is clear this largest retailer has gotten to be there because they have cut their expenses, and that means cutting staff to the bone. I do not expect to find someone with the time, let alone the patience, to answer all my picky questions in great detail. We have very little time as I approach a shy-looking, quiet young woman behind the camera counter and ask her for help.

I communicate my mental list of needs to the young saleswoman as follows: First, I do not want to spend much money; second, I want something small enough to fit in my pocket easily; and third, I need a camera that an idiot could learn to operate in five minutes. The word idiot is not used, but the idea is conveyed. The young woman's name is Vivian, and she is an unexpected pleasure to work with. She spends about twenty-five minutes pulling all the cameras out, letting me hold them and try them. She also goes to a discount shelf to search for others. They all seem too complex. Finally, it is apparent that getting a reasonable digital camera would cost a little more than I had anticipated spending. Vivian is patient and continues to work with me. We find one that seems right, and she lets me practice taking her picture. She loads it with a card and checks the batteries, and I get ready to pay for it with my credit card. (Note: Also a must is to have one's own credit card for emergencies or irresistible purchases.) This totals about $150 or so, and I am glad to have the camera. Vivian then pulls a camera case off the wall and adds it to the pile. When I ask her how much it is, she says just to take it, it is going to be reduced in price anyway. It is her way of expressing thanks for our coming to Louisiana to help.

Susan now comes over with an assortment of toys she is buying and needs to get in line at the front of the store. Looking at the daunting lines up front, it becomes apparent that twenty more precious minutes will be chewed up. Vivian says she will take the sale at her register and save us the time. Once again, it is her way of extending herself to say thank you to us.

People say thank you in so many ways. Some walked up to us and simply said "thank you." Some never said the words but extended a small kindness. For so much of this time in the South it was the simple, quiet, subtle, and unexpected gracious deeds that were extended that were so appreciated. Again, it was a reminder of how little it really takes to soften the harsh realities that tragedies in life can bring. In this case it turned out that this quiet, shy young woman who addressed us as "ma'am" all the time, was the manager. She had some advantages as a manager. Because of her position she was able to offer us more, and sure enough she used that advantage to extend herself. By the way, did I mention we had our Red Cross vests on? The community continued to show us an extension of thanks in so many small ways whenever they noted the Red Cross presence.

Somewhere around this time the thought occurred to me to keep a Red Cross shirt in the trunk of my car back home, to be whipped out whenever there was a need to feel cared about and appreciated. Unfortunately, the farther away from the actual disaster we got, the fewer were the expressions of appreciation. At the end of the trip back in California it was back to normal, and clerks were less than impressed about what was worn. No doubt some mathematical calculation can be developed to illustrate this point. There must be a correlation for the amount of distance from disaster as it relates to care expressed by the community. The further away I got from the disaster, the less the expression.

Sue and I are finally on our way and only get lost for about an hour this time. On the way up we pass huge military convoys heading back in the opposite direction. Cars pass and they honk at the convoys and give them high fives out the windows. We think they are headed for New Orleans. Large mobile homes and vans labeled "Homeland Security" go by, and we see many convoys of trucks that are going out to repair electricity. It is unlike any traffic we've ever seen before. There are police and military personnel everywhere. It does not feel like any semblance of normal life. I cannot help but wonder if this is what life would look like if we were at war.

We are on our way to Monroe. The town is several hours north of Baton Rouge. There is a shelter there, a huge sports arena called the Monroe Civic Center, where we will work. As we travel along the highway to Monroe we spot beautiful fields of growing cotton. We decide to stop at one to take some photos, and Sue takes a photo of me with the cotton. It is a gorgeous field with sunset beginning to color the sky. A beautiful black woman and man are driving by in a van, and they stop to see the cotton. The woman gets out of the car to see the cotton, and we learn that this couple has just come from New Orleans. The young woman has never seen cotton grow. Sue takes the time to talk with her about the experience of getting out of New Orleans.

Later, back in the car, Sue and I talk about the fact that this young woman who is black and living in southern Louisiana has never seen cotton grow. I think about my biases and about how I expected her grandparents or great-grandparents must have known what cotton fields looked like and how I assumed she would have seen them, too. I'm glad she never has seen cotton growing. I'm surprised, and I hope she was spared some of the injustices of our history. She stopped to pick a piece of cotton and take it home with her just as Sue and I did. I think again about my biases.

It is late when we get to Monroe. Again we get lost as we try to find the civic center. How hard could that be? It is a huge sports stadium in the center of town. Everyone knows it. The townspeople we ask all give us directions and we get lost again. By now we have learned to go to the police, but it is Sunday night and the city is empty. As we get closer to downtown we notice that no one is out; we don't see police or anyone else. The town is deserted. We drive around and accidentally find the police department. We are only blocks away from the center.

At last we are really here. The military is everywhere. We go through a checkpoint before entering the grounds. We have our IDs, and our car is clearly marked with a Red Cross sticker. We are waved through. More police and military are inside the building.

Finally, we get inside and wait to meet with our supervisor. She is a beautiful young woman with auburn hair, and she is managing some form of crisis as we sit watching her. We wait for twenty-five minutes to speak with her. She appears stressed, and I wonder what it will be like working for her.

Later I will learn she is fantastic. She is a beautiful, vibrant, energetic woman with vast experience. She can pick up a crying infant, and then soothe someone in a psychotic state in a flash. Faster than a speeding bullet, she easily puts her arms around anyone and calms them in a way that seems so effortless. She is so skillful; I wish I could be around her in real life. She can set limits and knows how to stop the ramblings of a woman in a manic state. I will be in awe later during this week as I watch her work. Her name is Debbie. She is here as a supervisor, but it is with amazement that I watch her in the trenches using her clinical skills.

Sue and I have only a moment with her. Debbie points to another volunteer, a young woman still in school at Davis University, who is in charge of organizing things. Debbie delegates well. The young woman is putting data on a spread sheet and organizing some of this chaos on a computer. Debbie delegates to this young woman the job of helping us find a place to sleep. Since we are so far north, most of the Red Cross volunteers will be local, and therefore they do not need a place to stay. This has freed up motel rooms. We have a good chance of being able to stay at a motel instead of sleeping at a shelter. Some of the luckier evacuees are staying at these same motels too. The town is filled with Red Cross volunteers and evacuees.

As usual, we get lost several more times before finding the motel. Sue and I are a good team and I enjoy being with her as a roommate. She is compassionate, patient, doesn't smoke, eats healthy food, works out at home, and has an admirable lifestyle. She calls her husband daily to keep in touch. She is always willing to help me learn the system. We are both directionally challenged. We are a disaster on the highway. We need an obsessive-compulsive, controlling, management-type volunteer to complement our lack of driving skills. At one point it seemed possible that all the flood waters in all the regions would recede and the entire crisis would be over before we would find our way to our motel.

I think about suggestions to make to my supervisor when we debrief at the end. We may be asked what we might change if we had it to do over again. I would emphatically ask that a Global Positioning System be installed in each rental car. At least if Sue and I ever pair again we would need this. I'm sure those of us who donate money to the Red Cross would be thrilled to know that the money was used for GPS help. Again, diplomacy prevails and I decide it is probably better to say nothing.

Tonight we have real mattresses and a private bath. I still sleep only about three or four hours. Tomorrow we will actually start to do what we came here to do, to provide mental health services. This is how things work in crisis. They are not smooth, they are frustrating, it is not efficient, and it takes too long to do simple things. This work is not for everyone. For me, however, it is the experience of a lifetime.

Chapter 7

The Sheltered Life

TODAY IS SEPTEMBER 5, Labor Day. It is the day we begin working in the Monroe Civic Center in Monroe, Louisiana. This shelter is a stadium, a large sports arena capable of holding thousands of fans. Once again Sue and I pass through the military checkpoint. Again the National Guard waves us through. We enter the building and sign in. We are given white wristbands. Volunteers wear white bands, resident evacuees wear red bands. I suddenly think about prison. The subtle bands differentiate us.

I am to work in the mental health unit. Part of my job is to diffuse potential violence, part is to assess for serious mental illness, helping those who might need refills for medication, and so on. Most of the time it will be to console, to comfort, to locate resources, to validate, to reassure people, and to establish a sense of hope. Most of the time people only need to be reassured that they are not crazy, that this is a crazy-making time and crazy-making situation.

Though the residents can leave anytime they want to, they have nowhere to go. They know it and we know it. In a sense they really are prisoners of this current event. They are innocent victims of this disaster. The residents have done nothing wrong, yet their power has been stripped from them. They do not have money; they do not have many choices, whereas I can leave at any time.

No matter how many hugs I can give, how much listening I can do, how much empathy I can express, no matter how much is provided in food and clothing, no matter how much I can try to engage residents, they know they cannot leave. There are currents of resentment and anger from a few of the residents toward me as I walk the halls saying hello. There are two clear cultures: those who have and those who don't. Sadly, for the most part, the residents are black and the volunteers are Caucasian. It has the appearance and is reminiscent of a racial divide all over again.

The National Guard is in every corridor. I know the guards are here for safety. They will keep the drugs, the alcohol, and the violence out. I am glad they are here, but it is clear the guards are here to watch the residents and not to watch the staff or the volunteers. There is an underlying presumption and aura here that the victims of this disaster bear watching. It might be no different having police patrol the streets in any large city, but somehow this presents a different dynamic. I wonder what it would be like to live under constant surveillance.

I am surprised there is so little anger expressed. Perhaps this is because it has been so short a time since the hurricane happened. It has been such a short time since the shelter was established here. Perhaps people are too intimidated to express their fear, their anxiety, and their rage. Perhaps some of them are still numb. Still there are signs of simmering resentment. There are eyes that won't look at me. They continue talking to each other and ignore me when I ask how things are, when I say hello. It is subtle, but it is clear.

Still, I am excited to be here. I'm eager to meet the people, to hear the stories, to be of comfort. I'm not sure if there will be violence or if I can defuse the anger, but I'm eager to try. Perhaps my exuberance is annoying to some who are saddened and depressed over their losses. I try to monitor it.

Sue and I have been assigned to a supervisor from national headquarters. His name is Sheldon. He has a Ph.D. in psychology. What were the chances that I would come to a Southern state that is deeply immersed in Baptist, Methodist, and Christian faith to find a Jewish supervisor? Of the thousands of people in Texas and Louisiana whom I have met, I've not knowingly met any person who was Jewish. Somehow, it did not matter. I always felt at home. Back home, upon meeting new people, the conversation inevitably turns to what your occupation is, where you live, how many children you have. A kind of social rating system often ensues. Here, I rarely find that to occur or for that information to be of any importance. Titles, occupations, income levels may be of some interest, but they are clearly unimportant here.

Sheldon is from California. He is retired and has vast experience. Sheldon has a beard and a mustache and reminds me of Freud. One of the volunteers has already affectionately dubbed him Siggy. Though Sheldon is technically our supervisor, and he is from national headquarters, he quickly tells us we are to report to Debbie and follow what she says. Debbie is the local volunteer and she has been in charge of setting up the mental health unit at the civic center from the beginning. Sheldon takes a background role. He has noticed that Debbie is extraordinarily capable. She lives in the community, and she knows the people and the resources. Sheldon is not on a power trip and does not need to run the show. He already has the experience and confidence to know his abilities. He does not have to prove himself to anyone. His self-esteem is not dependent upon anyone reporting to him. I admire him and discern that he is very wise. There are too many other agencies that do not work well together because of internal power struggles. Our mental health unit will all work well together this week.

I am not sure what we will find. Will there be a lot of anger, fear, or violence? There are so many strangers living in tight quarters, having to share bathrooms and meals, having to wear old donated clothing from other people, and sleeping on narrow cots made up with blankets and sheets once belonging to others. There are so many unknowns. There is absolutely no privacy. There are no newspapers, and TV is very limited. A few people have brought radios or tiny portable TVs that they keep plugged in. They usually sit off in some corner where they can be alone. There is some news on a big screen in one room and one or two other small TVs.

In general it is good not to traumatize children by showing images of destruction over and over again. It is a hard balance to play between allowing people the right to see and hear news and wanting to protect the young children from these continual scenes. The event happened once and the constant projections for weeks on the screens make it appear to be ongoing. The images themselves are traumatizing. It is hard for the adults to find a way to watch TV without the children present. They need someone else to care for the children, someone to protect their children from the ongoing, agonizing images, while they try to watch TV and attempt to absorb the meaning of this event.

There are so many uncertainties, and they take a great emotional toll. Have family members and friends survived? Will people be able to go back home? Will they have jobs? Will there be school? I wonder how Steve and I would fare if he lost his business, if I lost my job, if we did not know if David and Michelle were alive, if we had no idea if there would be money to start again, if I had to wonder how long until I could use a bathroom in private, or eat foods I liked. What would it be like to have no control over my life? What would it be like to have guards constantly walking around every part of the building where I lived? What would it be like to see armed guards where I slept, ate, used the bathroom, and went outside for fresh air? What would it be like to not know when this would end? In spite of all this trauma, I am pleased to find there is generally a sense of quiet and calm.

Susan and I start with a tour of the facility. We don't know exactly how many people are here today. There is no exact record. Residents leave and sometimes do not tell anyone they are leaving. There is not a good computerized system for entering data with who has checked in, where they are from, how many people are in their family, and so on. It all appears to be done by hand. This is still chaos we are dealing with—this is not a corporate setting with a sense of permanence. There is one large room to house all the departments. There are six-foot knockdown tables, folding chairs, computers, phones, and faxes in one room, but there are no real offices. The staff is doing the best they can. We are all volunteers and we change every few days. Training and re-training are constants. Supervisors change, volunteers change, residents change. It is easy to criticize and become frustrated. It is hard for those outside the system to see the difficulties faced and the dedication so many volunteers are demonstrating.

Susan and I start our tour at the main arena in the stadium. There are cots all over the place. They are lined up in rows down the center, and more cots are lined up against all the edges of the arena. There is absolutely no privacy. We are told that the stadium housed somewhere between 800 to 1,200 residents last week. There are other large rooms off the main corridor. Some are for families, some for couples. They are a little more private but still have about fifty or so people in each room.

The stadium has many bathrooms that normally are used for fans attending sporting events. Again, there is no privacy. There are huge gallon jugs of blue disinfectant hand-washing soap at the sinks. There are large handwritten notes pasted on the mirrors and walls, including notes urging everyone to wash using the disinfectant.

There are two nursing stations, along with a pharmacy that dispenses all prescribed medications free of charge beginning at nine thirty every morning. Residents begin lining up at nine to have their prescriptions filled. The pharmacy is staffed by and has been provided by Wal-Mart. For all my prior critical comments, I also must extend kudos to Wal-Mart for the help they have provided to the community. It is heart-warming to see this expression of care. Indeed, they deserve recognition for the things they do that are right.

Medical doctors are housed in two large mobile units in the parking lot where they can examine patients in private. Guards are always stationed near the medical and nursing stations. There is a sense of calm and general patience as people wait for medical care. It is wonderful to know that no one has to be bussed anywhere for medical care or for medication. There are no long waits for care, and prescriptions are filled quickly. It is staffed by volunteer doctors and nurses. People seem genuinely pleased with the respectful care they are given. I feel reassured by the guards' presence and begin to wonder about the cost of providing the military presence. I wonder how long it will be before this becomes a political and economic issue.

There is a table where residents drop off their laundry and it is returned to them clean the next day. I am amazed at this detail and had never thought of this basic task, or how it would get done. For a moment I toy with the idea of asking them to do my laundry too. I decide better of this. The volunteers did not come here to do my laundry. By the end of the week, however, I'm down to nothing clean, and I use the sink to wash some underwear.

There are local barbers who have set up chairs lining the main halls. They give free haircuts and mustache trims. There is a delightful spirit of joviality. There is the warm banter associated with barber shops between those local barbers volunteering their services and the residents who have evacuated. It is a welcome bit of respite from the process of trying to find loved ones and figuring out a new direction in life. They are able to laugh with me as I comment on the trims being provided. "How about a little more off the side," I ask. The men laugh, knowing I know nothing about style, and I look like a schlep. (That's a Jewish term for an unkempt, sloppy-appearing individual.) At some point I lost my comb, and the fine-tooth combs provided by this shelter do not work on my thick hair. One day I resort to using a plastic fork to comb my hair after a shower. Somewhere I lost my elastic hair band and resort to tying my hair back with a latex glove. I wonder if I can turn this into a new fashion statement once I get home. Hmm . . . could I become a trendsetter, a fashion designer? I toy with asking the local volunteer barbers to cut my hair too. Again, I think better of this. They are not volunteering their time to style my hair.

I want so much to take photos. They would be priceless. I want so much to be able to record the row of chairs lining the hall with men sitting there having their hair cut. I want to take close-ups to show the faces of the barbers who are giving their time to help boost morale with this familiar barbershop ritual. This moment in time makes me think of what it might feel like to be in an old-fashioned small town community with men sitting around sharing stories and laughs.

I want photos of the mothers and grandmothers combing their daughters' and granddaughters' hair, carefully placing colorful plastic balls in the hair as they braid it.

I want to take a photo of the tall, thin, young father, who looks barely twenty years old, as he carries his new one-month-old baby daughter tenderly in his arms so his young wife can get some rest. He cuddles and nurtures her and I comment on the warm, affectionate, and giving manner he shows with his new child. Despite all the fears and doubts of the future, despite the intimidating models all around him, despite all his young male cousins jostling each other, this young man knows his role in life at this point and tries not to be intimidated. His cousins strut their bodies, they flex their biceps; they try to appear powerful in order to attract young women. These young adolescent males are going through mating rituals, attempting to look tough and macho. Despite all this going on and the lack of recognition he gets from his family for his role in caretaking, this young father takes the time and uses his energy to show quiet, mild, and gentle loving care to his young infant daughter.

I want photos of the grandmother who is surrounded by a dozen grandchildren and her grown children. She is so cheerful. She is wearing a bright pink muumuu, the loose Hawaiian-style dress flowing easily over her figure. She lets me hold the newest infant in her family. The baby is her latest grandchild, barely two months old. This grandmother has lost all her possessions, and I ask her how she is getting through this. She says she cannot understand why others are so angry. "We have food, all we want; we have clothes. What do these people expect?" she asks. She is cleaning the table after she has eaten. She is very much overweight, has diabetes, and walking is difficult for her. Her smile is so genuine and she is such a joy to engage with. "How do you get through this time?" I ask. "I have Jesus," she says. "I know he will look after me."

I know and respect the importance of the right to privacy and confidentiality for those who enter the shelter. Photos are not allowed inside the shelter. I will try to be content with a written memory, but there is such a yearning to capture these images on film. I want to be able to have them so as to never forget. Instead, I decide to take photos of the volunteers, with their permission. Everyone is delighted. The military pose, the policewoman poses, the nurses are engaging and they pose. Other volunteers smile. In general they all want their photos taken. They ask for copies to be sent and hand me their e-mail addresses. Only one volunteer is irate, a man about seventy years old who works in the staff break room keeping the snacks organized. He says we are not to take photos, and I think he will report me. I tell my supervisor who humors me and says that guy is probably wanted in at least four states.

At the main entrance there are many computers. They are used for locating missing persons, attempting to get help registering with FEMA, and so forth. This area is always completely filled. Many people do not know how to use a computer, and there are Red Cross volunteers who sit with them to help. There also are phones where free calls may be made. These too are always full.

One of the most important things provided here is food, and there is such an abundance provided twenty-four hours a day. In the morning there are all kinds of juices, milk, cereals, breads, muffins, and fruit. There is never a limit to the amount of snacks one could take. Only occasionally do I see children take two Pop-Tarts or suckers at one time. In general there is great comfort in knowing there will be sufficient food at all times. This provides assurance regarding the future. For someone who has lost everything to now know they could be provided this most basic need in whatever quantity they want, at whatever time they want it, the value is enormous. It is a strong aid to the knowledge that there is hope and things will get better. There is a huge array of toaster pastries (cinnamon, apple, strawberry, and blueberry), lollipops, chips, macaroni and cheese, tacos and cheese, instant noodle soups, and candy bars. All kinds of junk foods are here.

Of course coming from Northern California with a background in teaching nutrition, I do think about the overabundance of sugar and fat being provided. I carry some relatively healthy cereal bars brought from home in my jacket pocket to take to children while I wander the halls. Occasionally, one will be taken by a child and tasted. It is always given back to me. Sometimes a child will take a bite before giving it back, other times it is just refused. Of all the times I try to give a child a cereal bar I cannot remember even one that is eaten. It is clearly an indication of how many highly sugared foods have been in their diets for many years, and the cereal bars are not sweet enough to appeal to the children. Nor do they have colorful cartoon characters on the packages. They simply do not have appeal in this market. Adults sometimes take one but generally only if they've had nothing else to eat as when they first drive up from outside the shelter and have no food. I remind myself that this is not the best or only time to develop good nutritional education. It is a time to comfort by providing familiarity. It is again a demonstration that comfort foods are those that are high in carbohydrates, sugars, and fats, those that take little effort or time to chew or digest, those that soothe and fill tummies quickly and cheaply. I worry about the habits of poor nutrition being encouraged again, and I console myself by deciding that not everything can be addressed in the midst of chaos. The priority is to feed, to sustain life. The fact that there is choice and abundance is a bonus. Nutrition education will wait. This is the time for sustaining life and for comforting, not for educating, but still I am going to try. The rate of diabetes is so high in this part of the country that several of the local registered nurses working here indicated the numbers were in excess of fifty percent. Steve would be in heaven here. He would not have to tolerate my tofu burgers, home grown fresh tomatoes, and organic, nonfat, hormone-free yogurt.

Another one of the many wonderful things happening here has been the huge outpouring of the community in their provision of food for the volunteers. Some is provided by the Red Cross. By far the donations from the community are the most appreciated for the local variety and taste. There are many daily deliveries of food from restaurants, businesses, and individuals for Red Cross volunteers, for lunch, snacks, and for dinner. Platters of sandwiches, tinfoil pans of spaghetti, salads, donuts, cookies, brownies, breads, and so on arrive daily. Most often there is no way to know who provided the food. It is not labeled, and there are often no business cards or flyers. It is an unselfish giving with rarely a thought of getting recognition for their gestures. The food just keeps coming and is so welcome. I remain touched by the generosity of this community in Monroe. On one morning a well-dressed woman came to the staff desk with two huge platters of freshly baked brownies. She apologized and said she could not stay. She was a local resident, an attorney on her way to court that morning. Still, she found time for this caring gesture.

Another wonderful addition is the toys that are donated. Individuals and companies send toys, books, puzzles, bubbles, crayons, coloring books, plastic toy cars, dolls, stuffed animals, balls, larger plastic toy trucks to ride on, and other toys. In one section off the main lobby, a room was set up to serve as a toy store. It has those Dutch doors that open on the top and bottom, with a counter in the middle, and children of all ages can come there anytime during the day and get whatever they want. They learn they can each have things for themselves and that some things have to be shared. There is an abundance of toys. Again, this is a message that indicates there will be enough for you, there will be a future, there is time for fun, and the world will be okay. In the halls there are drawings, cards, and letters the children have made. There is a mini art gallery lining the walls in the main hall. It is a signal that the children's work is worthy of display and that they are worthy of recognition.

On this Labor Day there is suddenly a loud sound of music in front of the civic center. A high school band has come to play. It is delightful. Some of the residents have come out to hear the music, and some of the young children came outside and spontaneously began to dance. This is another reminder that there will be fun again and that high school students have had a part in sharing their time to provide some cheer. It is as important for the local students from the town's high school, those who have not suffered the losses personally, to learn and feel the value of sharing as it is for those from New Orleans who experienced the losses. This is definitely a lesson on demonstrating compassion—cheers to the school and its staff for taking the role in educating beyond the classroom curriculum. What an excellent way to teach compassion.

Work the Crowd

AFTER GETTING THE general overview of the civic center, I decide it would be best to follow Sheldon around the facility to get a better idea of how he works. This is my first major national disaster assignment, and I'm eager to learn from a professional who has done this before. I follow him into the main arena. This is the stadium playing field. It is where star athletes play and now hundreds of cots fill the room. I wonder if any of these children will one day be athletes and play in this center.

Will it evoke memories of this time? Will this be a flashback of trauma, or will it provide memories of attempts to provide comfort. I hope it will provide good memories of a time that provided images of hope.

It is early morning. Most of the cots are empty and residents are in all parts of the stadium. Sheldon walks up and down the rows. He stops at one where there is a young man in his mid-twenties. Sheldon kneels down and positions himself to the side of the cot and begins a conversation. He is lower than the young man. This position is sometimes referred to as the one-down position. It is a less threatening physical position to be in and works extraordinarily well in this setting. It is one at which Sheldon is a master. He never threatens anyone with his knowledge or position. It helps him with residents, staff, and authorities. Over the years it can take a toll on one's knees, and flexibility is a must. I don't have enough time to follow Sheldon a great deal but it is quickly apparent that he has the uncanny ability to spot those people who will need mental health assessments. He can spot those who need help almost instantly by just walking through a room filled with hundreds of people. On this day Sheldon spots a young man who has remained in his cot with the sheet over his head. He may have been under the sheet for days. He remained in his cot, fearing to venture out. I never did learn if he had much of anything to drink or eat during those days in the shelter. Sheldon was able to engage him, assess for serious mental illness and determine whether a psychiatric consultation and medications were needed. Sheldon set the model for showing compassion and respect for all those with whom he worked.

Soon after this brief tour, Sheldon tells us to roam the facility checking out residents, talking with staff, volunteers, police, and the National Guard. The volunteers generally know to come to us if they see anything unusual. He says to go "work the crowd." This is the basic, informal, and very hands-on and effective way to prevent problems by being aware of potential issues before they become major difficulties. This is the way we work on a daily basis. In hospitals it would be similar to making rounds.

At this point I am hyped, feeling good, ready to begin, consciously feeling ready to tackle the day. I can do anything, I think. Underneath there are still concerns about what will be there, out on the floor. Will there be violence, will there be drugs or alcohol, will there be any acting out of the rapes, murders, and suicides that have been briefly alluded to in the media in New Orleans? Will this ever be presented here? These thoughts are not consciously in my mind, but subconsciously there are certainly some alarming concerns.

As I prepare to begin to walk the floor on my own I need to use a bathroom. Immediately walking inside the first bathroom in the hall, I am met inside by my supervisor Sheldon. "Annette, did you know you were in the men's room?" he asks. I had no idea, no clue, never looked at any signs, or if I did see them I did not read them. This is a sign to me that my anxiety level is out of order. It was high. Fortunately, Sheldon never seriously considers me as too weird and he is able to laugh with me about it long after. Anxiety was simply to be a part of the experience whether it was conscious or not.

Paper Clips

DURING THE 9-11 event in 2002 in New York, the Red Cross mental health volunteers found that many people became upset when they realized a mental health worker was called to be with them. Both victims and staff sometime interpret this as if there is something wrong with them mentally, that they are crazy or incompetent. Needless to say, they do not want to talk with a counselor. The mental health volunteers decided that they would have to identify themselves in a way that did not alarm anyone. It was thereafter decided to wear a small, unobtrusive, and barely noticeable paperclip near one's collar to distinguish oneself as a mental heath volunteer.

One day during this event in Louisiana, an evacuee came to a new volunteer and said in a loud and urgent voice, "I need a paper clip!" The new volunteer hurriedly searched the table and left for a moment, saying she would be right back. Sure enough, she came back after some searching and handed the resident a large paper clip. "No, no you %^&*, I need a *paper clip*, I need a person!" The resident knew she wanted a mental health counselor. The volunteer did not.

So much for the system of trying to protect the residents from knowing that mental health workers were among them and for the notion that the residents would be alarmed by seeing a counselor. Apparently these residents did not need protection from the idea that mental health counselors were being called only for crazy folks. We could be identified easily and many residents knew exactly what the paper clips represented. So much for having volunteers who didn't get every ounce of training, and who did not know the history or the meaning or symbolism of a paper clip. This volunteer did not know what a paper clip signified. So what? There were many volunteers who did not know what the clip meant. Sometimes we think we need to protect others when, indeed, we don't realize their strength and abilities and that they may not really need our protection. There were many of these moments of humor along the way.

At times in the civic center shelter the staff will call over the loudspeaker, "A paper clip is needed at the nurses' station," or the main lobby, or some other location where the need is. Sometimes it is an urgent call. This reminds me of the classic TV show, *M*A*S*H*, which humorously depicted our United States Army often bumbling along while trying to manage numerous crises at the same time One day in particular it felt like Monroe was a mini mental health MASH unit. So many crises were occurring at exactly the same time.

For starters, there was an elderly woman in a wheelchair who had just been brought in by a relative. He was a man in his late forties, and by the level of concern he expressed I surmised he must have been her son. She was sitting in the front lobby directly in front of me. She was having chest pains and perspiring heavily. It looked like a possible heart attack, and she was clearly in great urgent medical danger. Though there was hardly a social work procedural manual to describe how to handle this type of situation it was clear we needed someone with medical expertise immediately. A microphone was nearby. I learned where the on and off buttons were (remember I'm a techno klutz), I picked it up and called the paramedics to immediately come to this location. They arrived in moments and it was a great relief to know there were doctors with offices in trailers in the parking lot just outside the building.

A minute or two later there was an interaction with a very young, very well-endowed woman dressed scantily in a tank top that looked as if it would fall off in a breeze or if someone nearby sneezed. She was complaining of being cold while she waited in an air conditioned interview room to be considered for referral for psychotropic medications. She needed a blanket for her shoulders or she might refuse to sit still and wait for the interview. Of course all these events were happening at the same time and in different parts of the building. We did not have a courier service for blankets so we each did whatever was needed. Blanket running was my assignment at that moment.

While running for a blanket, at exactly this same time, a volunteer stopped me and wanted to talk about another volunteer who she thought was crazy and who needed to be taken out (out as in off duty, not annihilated). She was upset about the way he was serving cereal to the children (?) . . . never did get to follow up on that one. Having once worked in a hospital where they used the term triage, I determined this one would not be the priority. How serious could poor cereal service be? There were of course issues about the volunteer who thought this was a major concern, but that would also have to wait.

Jay and His Family

ON THIS SAME day and again at just about the same time as these other events were happening, over the loudspeaker an urgent call was put out several times "We need a paper clip at Nursing Station Two! We need a paper clip at Nursing Station Two!" Several of us literally ran across the stadium to the nursing station. We arrived to find two National Guardsmen ready to restrain a tall, muscular boy who was beginning to yell and on the verge of getting out of control physically. I will call him Jay. Jay was refusing to take his medication. He had been taking medications at home in New Orleans for years to control his aggressive behaviors. He was big and appeared to be about fifteen or sixteen years old. Actually, Jay was just eleven. With the prodding of his mother, and after seeing the guards surround him, Jay decided to take his medication.

I left the area, and then returned a few minutes later to see how he was doing. By now Jay was sitting on his cot alone. His head was down, he was nonverbal. I knelt down beside him, as Sheldon had modeled, and asked if it was okay to sit near him. He nodded yes. Jay allowed me to gently touch his shoulder. He was fighting back tears and allowed me to continue to touch his shoulder. Jay did not speak, he could only nod in agreement as I suggested this was a very difficult time and must be frightening. He never spoke. I later found out he did not like taking medication because it gave him a headache. Soon his mother, Jean, appeared and sat on the cot next to us. She was less than five feet tall and probably weighed no more than ninety pounds. She was very quiet and appeared so frail. Jean and I spoke for the next half hour or so while Jay went off by himself.

Over the next few days Jean and I would meet informally for a few minutes to talk. She wanted to talk so much but had no one to talk with and quietly kept her pain inside. She shared her past with me and stated she had been abused repeatedly by her husband. Her teeth had been knocked out, and her husband now was incarcerated. Jay had been sexually molested by his father. As I observed Jay he was coloring in a book that was more appropriate for a six- or seven-year-old. Jay appeared to be functioning intellectually at a much lower level than his eleven years. He hated school and had been taunted there continually. Jay and his mother were both here with a very large extended family of cousins, uncles, and aunts. He constantly fought with his cousins, both verbally and physically.

Jay's cot was barely two feet from his mother's cot. His cousins were all in a row within a few feet of each other. They desperately needed some separation. Jay functioned much better when he had some space to himself, yet when I suggested that his cot could be moved a few feet across the hall, still within sight of his mother, he declined. She was his only protector and he wanted to be close to her in the dark of night.

The trauma of having lost all their possessions, being uprooted, and living in very tight quarters made this situation a powder keg ready to explode. Employment in the future was unknown for his adult male cousins, making this a very anxiety-provoking experience. There was a new infant in this extended family, and several other young cousins about four or five years old to provide for. The family had not learned healthy coping skills in the past. They used verbal abuse, threats, and violence to deal with the world and each other. The current situation was ripe for the continuance of physical abuse. Jay was being medicated to control his anger, and his medication had been changed a few months before this flood. Jean was trying so hard to keep peace in the family. She was being blamed by the rest of the family for her son's behavior. The rest of the family believed that all Jay needed was some "tough love, a good whomping now and then." His mother was seriously depressed but had not resorted to drugs or alcohol; her only addiction was cigarettes.

Jean was afraid to go back to work because she had no teeth and knew she could no longer work as a receptionist. She had no money to have her teeth repaired. The family did not talk to her. Jean felt all alone. The needs in this family were enormous. Jean and I were just developing a relationship and some trust when I learned the shelter was going to close down and move. I was due to leave the next morning to return home to California. Trauma upon trauma was occurring. I went to see Jean on the morning of the shelter move. She was sitting on the sidewalk smoking cigarettes. Jay was refusing to go to school. The National Guardsmen were back again near Jay in the parking lot watching him and fearing he might be getting ready to be out of control again.

The good fortune was that we had a fantastic young male therapist who lived and practiced in town. Ronnie was volunteering today. He was able to go with me to meet Jay and his mother and could provide the much needed skill and continuity of care if the family remained in Monroe. He provided a wonderful model as a much needed healthy male figure for both Jay and Jean. Ronnie could follow the family in counseling if they stayed in Monroe. They had such a need for some structure and stability.

Ronnie came with me to meet Jay and his mother. He was such a natural. In another setting we would have been called co-therapists. Here it just seemed so natural and easy, as if we were simply friends talking and working together. Ronnie knelt down next to Jay and started talking with him. He was an excellent therapist. Ronnie had a good background in family therapy and I could tell he would be wonderful. In a few minutes Jay easily agreed to walk with Ronnie to get a snack.

While they walked off Jean and I were able to talk alone. She was now deep in tears and seriously depressed. She had no one she could talk with and needed support to be able to move forward in her life. Jean agreed she would go for counseling with Jay, which could be established here in Monroe. Ronnie would be able to follow up with them while they lived in Monroe.

This was the high point of my professional experience in Louisiana. When I think of what good could come of this disaster, it is the fact that this family would have continued in their destructive, helpless, and depressed manner if they had not found a good therapist along the way. Jay was being medicated, but the problems were not being addressed. He was being blamed for all the problems in the family. He was the identified patient. He was absorbing the blame for all the difficulties, frustrations, and anger in this situation, and for other events in their lives. In short, Jay was a scapegoat.

We do this in society when we find one individual or one minority group to focus on. It is faster and seems easier than addressing the more complex problems. We blame all our economic problems or other issues on one group. We focus and vent our hostility in one place. It releases tensions. Some healthier ways are thought to be through athletics. At least here the participants have a choice and often get well paid for their efforts. Football, wrestling, hockey, and other sports are some of the most revered endeavors in our culture. They serve the same function, to be an outlet for emotions and to release energy. Jay, of course, was not offered the luxury of choice or compensation for taking these blows.

At this point both Jay and Jean said they were willing to enter counseling to learn new coping mechanisms and to improve their lives. I was due to leave for California early that next morning but decided I wanted to stay a while longer to be with this family and others through this move to the new facility. My presence could provide some brief continuity at the new facility. They could have just one more familiar face when they arrived. But, honestly, it was as much for my own comfort as it was for theirs. I needed to know they had made it okay.

In my pocket were a handful of Mardi Gras beads. Steve had them at home in the garage. They were left over from a long-ago party, and I had brought them with me thinking there might be an occasion to use them here. This was that time. There were three female relatives, mothers with young children, traveling with Jay and Jean to the new facility. I asked them if they would like to have the beads, thinking maybe this was silly. This was one of the groups of women who previously would not talk with me as I walked through the halls. This time they all wanted the beads and eagerly put them on to prepare for the trip to the new shelter. For the moment these bright, shiny plastic beads were like real jewels. They served as a reminder of more festive times and symbolized better times ahead.

Though the shelters were only a few miles apart, it took many hours to make the move from one shelter to the other. There were 800 to 1000 people moving, including staff and volunteers. It was definitely chaos, but an organized, caring kind of chaos if that is conceivable. Still this was another high point for me. Out of all the places I needed to be that day of the move, it so happened that I was inside the entrance of the new building when Jean's family came through the line. Their possessions all were traveling through an X-ray conveyer belt and each person had to be scanned with a wand by a security guard when they came into the building. They had their shiny beads on, and I instinctively reached out and hugged them all as they came through the line. They seemed much like a family at an airline terminal when a plane lands. This time the previously hostile adult women accepted the hugs and even briefly and fleetingly smiled back.

I worked that evening again from 10:00 p.m. to 5:00 a.m. and did not get to see the rest of this family again. I briefly saw Jay and Jean during the day but did not really connect with them. I was not able to stay in Louisiana to see the actual transition and continuance in therapy with Ronnie but was thankful that I was here in the moment when this family saw the opportunity to make their lives better, when they saw a better way, a hopeful future. It was a moment of joy. I had such pride about entering the field of social work with its potential to touch lives.

I trust that if they stayed with counseling, Jean would be able to get new teeth, get a job, and develop confidence in her ability to manage her life and find happiness. She was a very caring and sensitive woman who just wanted the best for her son. I am sure that Jean could discontinue being a victim and develop more assertiveness and strength. I trust that Jay would be able to attend school, be evaluated for developmental disabilities, and receive an appropriate education. I hope that the rest of the family might find jobs and homes, and become engaged in learning new better ways to interact and raise their young families.

I feel like such an optimist and can see the possibilities for such a wonderful future. These are just a few examples of the possibilities that great social work and psychology can bring to the world. There is such potential in our field to impact lives and our culture. We need to be included more in mainstream media, not just our own professional journals, in order to educate the public and elected officials regarding the role social work plays in improving lives. It is certainly cheaper than building and maintaining prisons.

The Scream

ON THE DAY before the move, at about the same time as Jay first became enraged, a volunteer came up to the mental health desk in a great hurry and said we need a paper clip immediately. I went with her to the front desk in the center of the main hall where people were signing up to enter the facility. A woman of about thirty was screaming and crying uncontrollably. She wanted money for a bus ride out of town to another state. She could barely speak, but she agreed to walk with me to a nearby seat, away from the center of the hall, where she simply disintegrated into tears as I put my arms around her. It was quite a few minutes before she was able to speak. I simply sat with her. Then she spoke. I do not recall her name, but I will call her Linda.

Linda spoke of living in New Orleans and of hearing the news about the hurricane. She said she had listened to the local news and never heard the message to evacuate. She was angry about that and felt she was not well informed by the officials. She was used to being prepared for emergencies. When she first learned of the potential for flooding,

Linda and her boyfriend had parked their car up on the highest hill in the neighborhood in the event they would have to leave.

On the first day after the flood, she went outside and the water was up to her ankles. She and her boyfriend, Mitchell, stayed and listened to the news. Nothing was heard about evacuating. The second day, the water was up to their knees. Nothing was heard about evacuating. On the third day the water was chest high, and they still heard nothing on the news about evacuating. She talked with Mitchell, and he said they had to leave, and they would have to swim to the car. They swam to where the car was. Though it was parked on the highest hill they could not find their car. Finally Mitchell said he knew where the car was. It was deep under the water where they were swimming. There was no way to use it. They swam back to the house, and Mitch said they would have to swim to other houses.

Linda and Mitch had two small dogs, and Mitch told her they would have a better chance of making it if they left the dogs at home. Linda talked of how she put out bowls of water for the dogs, and then cut up small pieces of meat and left them in different bowls in the kitchen. She planned to come back to them later. Today, at this moment, Linda was haunted by the face of one of her tiny dogs as she remembered putting her back down on the floor. She then left to swim to another house. Linda and Mitch swam for three days, back and forth to other homes. She met with her mother and remained on a rooftop with others who were waiting for helicopters to pick them up one at a time.

When the time came for Linda and Mitch to be picked up by the helicopter they gave up their spot to her mother, knowing that she was more fragile and could not withstand much more time on the roof. They did not really know when or if the helicopter would be back. Right now Linda was depressed by the realization she could not go back for her dogs. I don't recall the kind of dogs she had, but she described being haunted by the image of one of them, a small, fluffy, gentle and sweet puppy about a year or so old. Linda appeared inconsolable.

After about half an hour Linda started to calm down and said she had a sister living out of state but did not have money to get there. She wanted to know if the Red Cross could help her with transportation. I left her to see what I could find out and the next half hour was spent trying to find resources for travel. The Red Cross had no vouchers in place for transportation. The Salvation Army, which was providing transit in Baton Rouge, was not doing so here. The bus companies were filled to capacity and not providing free transit. FEMA was on the grounds but did not have anything set up. One woman volunteer, a local Monroe resident, had donated funds for transit but was so overwhelmed with needs she had no more funds.

I returned to Linda, indicating there was nothing in place yet. She would have to remain at this shelter a little while longer until the agencies had these funds in place. At least she would be safe here, and at least her boyfriend was with her, her mother was safe, and she had a sister they could go to. Over the next day or so Linda and I would briefly see each other in the hall. We would hug and she would be off. I stopped by to meet her boyfriend, and they seemed to be doing well.

He's Just a Spoiled Brat

ON ONE OF the mornings while walking through the halls, I was behind Mary, a young mother with a two-year-old son. I will call him John. He was running ahead, screaming and crying. She had been yanking at his little arms and clearly was stressed. Mary was screaming at him. John seemed unmanageable to her and she was exhausted from caring for him. "He's just a spoiled brat and needs the belt," she said. I had no doubt if she were back home that is exactly how Mary would have managed him. She looked so tired. I put my arms around her and said my typical phrases: "This is a tough time," "Kids take so much energy," and I just walked with her. We talked a little and I said she sounded like she needed a break. Mary was afraid John would not go to any stranger. She said he cried all the time and was afraid to be away from her. I offered to take him for a bit, picked him up in my arms, and walked ahead with him. Mary was able to see him the whole time, but John was not able to see his mother. So long as John did not see his mother, he was fine. The minute he saw her he started to cry again. Mary had interpreted this as John being a brat.

In fact John appeared to be much like any normal and typical two-year-old. He was scared; there were so many strangers; he was in a new setting; his sleep times were disrupted; the foods were new; his bed was different; his clothes, blankets, everything was different. John had no routine and nothing was familiar. It was normal that he would cry and want to be with the one person who provided familiarity. He was clinging to her all the time. Mary had no rest. She was young; this was her first child. She did not have family, friends, or a babysitter to give her a break. It was draining her energy.

John was running all over the halls. She could no longer keep up with him. Mary had no concept of what was normal for a two-year-old. She needed rest. She needed some awareness of normal child development and some skills for coping. Fortunately, we had some wonderful volunteers who would play with young children, read stories to them, and give parents a much-needed tiny bit of respite. Some of the volunteers were positioned in the middle of the huge arena on a great set of blue exercise mats, the kind gymnasts use. This was after all a sports arena where professional athletes played, and these were probably the actual mats that the athletes used. The volunteers had toys, puzzles, and books, and they played with the children. The parents had the option of staying in the arena and watching their children from a distance. Once the parents felt that their children were safe and the caregivers could be trusted, the parents would go off for an hour or so taking that much-needed break. It was wonderful for the children as they gained social skills, learned to rely on others and generally had fun. Some of the volunteers were teachers, some were college students, and some were mothers.

I made a deal with Mary. First, I indicated it was clear she really loved John and wanted to be a good mother. I told her I knew she did not want to hurt him, and that she was not going to do so. She would recognize when she was tired and needed time out. If she was really stressed and felt she could not tolerate John for another minute she would go to the nearest Red Cross volunteer, the nearest police officer, or the nearest National Guard person and say she could not care for him for another moment, and ask the person to please take him from her for now. There was so much staff, so many volunteers, police, and National Guard around that we were never more than a few feet away twenty-four hours a day. There was built-in daycare. Mary promised.

On one occasion Mary needed some medical care and was seen waiting in the clinic for a doctor. Needless to say, John, as any normal toddler, was not interested in sitting still for the half an hour or so it would take. He began squirming and crying. He had not yet had breakfast and was hungry. Mary would have lost her spot waiting in the clinic line if she had to go back to get him breakfast. I offered to get something and bring it back. She said he liked chocolate milk. As luck would have it they were out of chocolate milk, but I was able to find some Cocoa Puffs and milk. Mixing them together was as close as I was going to get to finding chocolate milk that morning. I brought that back to the clinic along with some Pop-Tarts, and he began to eat. My old nutrition professor at grad school, who may well be dead by now, would be turning over in her grave if she heard this.

As luck would have it there was a young mental health volunteer from a local college who was able to sit next to Mary and chat while she was waiting to be seen by a doctor. They talked about children in a very casual way and the volunteer was able to begin to share what normal child development was. It was a good beginning to developing some healthy parenting skills.

A day or so later Mary needed to go outside for something. She had John with her in his stroller. She saw me and asked if I could please watch him. Of course I took him but did not have a lot of time for babysitting. On that day at that same time there was a very official looking group of county and city officials in the building. They were being followed by TV cameras in an office off to the side of the main arena. Among the group of visitors in the building that day there was also a very well-dressed man in a business jacket and a woman in a business-type dress walking around the main lobby looking very congressional. They were not part of the other group but they both had official-looking name badges and were talking about the inefficiency of services in terms of FEMA and the Red Cross. They had no official role with the Red Cross and were local residents observing the scene to take information back to some committee or newspaper. I think they were with a school district but it definitely had the feel of politics.

Figuring they looked pretty safe, were not surrounded by any media at the time, and did not seem to be doing anything productive at the moment, I asked if they would watch a child for a few minutes until his mother came back. The man became a little concerned and asked how old the child was. He did not want to hold a young infant. I surmised he was afraid an infant might throw up or have an indiscreet event in a diaper, and this might mess up his suit. I figured they needed to do something more helpful than standing around being critical, and I wanted them to experience the actual process of helping. I motioned to Mary and told her these two official-looking folks would be right in the center of the hall, surrounded by the military, and they could watch John for a few minutes. There was no concern about them kidnapping any child. They would clearly be relieved if they could get rid of John as soon as possible. Of course John behaved beautifully as he always did when he was not able to see Mary. He sat quietly in his stroller, watching people bustling about in the main lobby. Feeling rather smug about getting these two folks to do some actual caretaking, I went back to work.

Over the next few days Mary was able to leave John for short times with others. During the remaining time at the shelter I never again saw Mary looking stressed with John. In fact, she seemed to be smiling and eagerly reached out for hugs whenever we met.

The Wild Ride

ONE OF THE daily responsibilities of the mental health supervisors was to continually be aware of and review anyone who might have serious psychiatric illness. This was good preventative care. Some might be in need of medications or refills for previously prescribed medications. On one morning during such a review it became apparent that Eric, one of the residents, could not wait until the next day to meet with an MD. Eric was a tall, very slim, gray-haired black man of about sixty-five or so. Although he was relatively calm at the present moment, he was constantly talking to himself and was not coherent. Much of his speech was not clear, which could have been due to years of taking medication. Some of his conversations involved Russian spies being around and the need to be wary of others.

The closest mental health clinic that could provide the medication by injection needed was a few miles away, and it would be open for only one more hour. The clinic did not make house calls. Sheldon, my supervisor, called the clinic and arranged an appointment. The only problem was transportation. It could have been arranged to have guards transport Eric, but that would have presented Eric with a show of force and unnecessarily alarmed him. He was paranoid enough already and had just begun to trust Sheldon. The fastest way to transport Eric was for Sheldon to drive Eric to the clinic himself. I became alarmed, thinking what if on the way there Eric really did become violent. It was agreed that I would accompany Sheldon by sitting in the backseat with Eric, and Sheldon would concentrate on driving to the clinic.

Eric was taller and stronger than I, but I had a bigger mouth. On the way there Eric talked constantly about sports, Russians, the army, his family, and lots of things I could not understand. Football was his favorite sport. All I could think about was keeping him talking constantly to distract him until we got to the clinic. I know nothing about sports other than a few names of players. "So what do you think about Steve Young, Jerry Rice, and Steve Mariucci?" I asked. (Steve Mariucci was a San Francisco 49ers coach who had once lived in our town, and I felt smug about knowing his name.) Though Steve was no longer the coach of the Niners, Eric was old enough to know his name. I asked Eric, "How about the Bears?" (we once had lived in Chicago), and then asked, "What do you think about the Refrigerator?" (a huge Chicago football player who played for the Bears some fifteen years ago and was nicknamed the Refrigerator because of his size). That was the extent of what I knew about football. I had regurgitated the only few names of sports figures I knew. Luckily, Eric was willing to talk endlessly about any of these names. We had a few more blocks to go and I wanted a pat on the back so I asked Eric how I was doing. "So for an old white lady how am I doing?" I asked Eric. I have no idea what he said, but we did engage and by now we were at the clinic and were greeted by a very tall and powerful-looking police officer at the door.

Once inside I thought this was going to be a piece of cake. The staff would immediately usher Eric in, give him his shot, it would work immediately, and we would be home free.

So much for what I know about how mental health clinics work. There were forms to fill out, IDs to show, and of course a wait. Sheldon handled the staff and the paperwork. His previous contact with the psychiatrist was to pay off by getting this process to be as smooth as possible.

In the meantime Eric had nothing to do. I got some paper and a pencil and we began to play dots. He showed me some other game called boxes that I could never figure out, but that was okay. Eric felt in charge and did not feel threatened by any aliens for the moment. He wrote some sentences, and we just kept having simple conversations about anything. I figured as long as he was talking it would be okay, and it was.

Eric saw the psychiatrist and both were charming with each other. The nurse, Sheldon, and I just sat there in the same room with them and all went well. Eric got his shot and his other medications to take back to the civic center. We had a pleasant drive back to the shelter.

When we got back Sheldon admitted to me he never considered Eric would be a risk on the drive. Eric was very compliant. I think Sheldon just let me come along for the ride. That was fine with me; it was an experience to remember. As I thought about it again, I realized that Sheldon would not have put my five-foot-one-inch torso in the backseat with a six-foot, potentially violent soul who was psychotic. I think it was just to have company . . . and maybe Sheldon didn't know as much about football as I did. I'm grateful Eric wasn't into ice hockey. Then there would have been real trouble. All I know is the name "Sharks."

Sheldon did pay me a compliment later that day. He said he thought I would work well with psychotics. I wonder if maybe I liked playing psychotic myself. Changing subjects, not staying on task, not having to make sense, talking all the time, acting much younger, playing games, it all has a certain appeal to me. The shot thing, however, is a different matter.

Changing of the Guard

By Wednesday I had become familiar with several of the residents and we had started to form some bonds. The next day our unit was told that the Monroe Civic Center would be closing as a shelter and the residents would all be moving. Using the civic center as a shelter was at a great financial cost to the civic center and probably involved a great loss of taxes for the city too. They could not do this for very long, and they needed to begin producing revenue again. A new building was found to serve as a shelter. A huge meeting for the volunteers was held in the auditorium to brief us about the process. A description of the new building was given and a discussion ensued about how the move was to take place. It was described as a much better place to be than the stadium. The new site was an office building that had originally housed the State Farm Insurance Company employees. It was all on one floor, there was a full cafeteria, and the bathrooms were much nicer. Then came the caveat: there were no showers. Residents would be bussed once a day to take showers. Sheldon was heard to say in a not-so-quiet voice: "What, no showers? Sign me up for the nearest pet shelter." He had a wonderful way with words.

While this move was understandable and necessary, it also would produce further trauma to the residents. They had been displaced from their homes, some of them several times before coming to Monroe. They finally began finding some familiar staff and volunteers, and now they would be moving again. Trauma upon trauma was occurring. I decided I would extend my stay at least through this move to provide some brief consistency to the families I had come to know. It was as important for me as it was for them. I needed to know they were adjusting as well as could be. I needed to see them to feel okay. I did not know how long I would stay. Debbie, our supervisor, suggested staying through the move, and then making a decision about how long I wanted to remain.

I called home and arranged it with my real day job, indicating I would be willing to take the time off without pay since my vacation had been used. The harder part was calling Steve, who wanted to know when I would be home. I asked him what the hardest thing was for him. "You never showed me how to run the dishwasher," he said. "So what are you doing? Are you washing the dishes by hand?" I asked. "No, I just break them," he said. There of course was no anger detected.

Our mental health unit was given a few hours on Thursday, the day before the move, to tour the new building. We would make the actual move on Friday. We were each given assignments as to what we would be responsible for during the move. I was in charge of orientation. The exact nature of what this meant was never even partially clear to me. The best I could figure out, it meant when the residents came to the new building I would be responsible for orienting them, which to me meant where they would sleep, where the bathrooms were, where the cafeteria was, where the desks for information on school, jobs, and so forth were. I knew there would be some help with that, but since there was no time to meet with other units and precious little time to spend planning, I surmised I had best know the building layout before the next day. I decided to make it my business to tour the building and memorize where the main areas were, including the bathrooms, sleeping areas, and cafeteria.

There were six of us in the mental health unit who drove together to visit the new building. It was a wonderful brick building, all on one level, very clean and modern, and seemingly would serve as a much better shelter than the stadium. The bathrooms had large counters and were far less institutional than those in the stadium. There was a huge lawn outside the building. The facility would eventually be able to house over 4,000 residents if needed in the future.

The building was fully carpeted, and the walls were painted, unlike the cold concrete cinderblock walls in the stadium. There were partitions in place designating where families, couples, single men, single women and those with disabilities would be settled. The carpeting had tape markers to designate how far apart cots would be placed. The high point was the incredible child care center. It had fabulous color, wonderful wood tables, slides, and bookcases stocked with many toys and books, and it was light and cheerful with photos on the walls. It would be staffed by well-trained volunteers whose profession was teaching, and it would rival any of the best private day care centers. It was so inviting I wanted to sit on the slide and play with the toys myself!

There would also be groups for parents to join that would educate families about child development. They would be valuable as they worked with issues on how to manage children during these particularly stressful times.

Just outside this area was a small room with a handwritten sign naming it the Cry Room. It had two adorable cribs, one was white and one was a beautiful, lively, bright pink. Rocking chairs were soon to be added. I immediately went inside to test it out by screaming and crying. I was quickly ushered out by someone who told me the room was not for staff or volunteers. This cleverly created area was for parents with infants who would cry during the night. They could go there with their infants to rock and soothe them. Since there were to be at least 800 or so other residents on the first night, this would permit the rest of the residents some semblance of quiet during the night.

A nursing station was in the building, and medical care was being provided along with a mental health department for assessments and counseling. There were other rooms for management of the facility and equipment. For all the comments about inadequacies and inefficiencies that one would hear over the days, it was clear that a lot of thinking, caring, and planning had been done. All efforts were made to make this as comfortable a shelter as possible. Everyone I met worked long hours and gave it 110%. Everyone volunteered their time, and most had regular jobs as well as their own families who needed their time too. They were good-hearted, generous, and compassionate people, and I was so fortunate to have the experience and pleasure of working with them.

This of course did not mean it was easy or smooth. Just before beginning the tour we were given a statistic about the building that meant little to me at the time. The building was reportedly 359,000 square feet which someone computed out to be eight acres. That was just the inside of the building, not including the grounds.

After getting the tour I decided I would walk the building again and map it out to prepare for being responsible for the orientation tomorrow. There were to be over 800 residents arriving on the next day, and as earlier stated my interpretation of being responsible for orientations was that I would be responsible for orientation. We had been given a floor plan the day before that I deftly whipped out to review. The floor plan had just that . . . a floor. There were no delineations for where bathrooms, cafeteria, walls, entrances, windows, doors, or north or south orientations were. It was ten minutes of hell when I once again became anxious and realized I couldn't find my way around. I was determined to put markings on this plan to determine where things were. For the next hour, while my colleagues were in a meeting, I decided I had best familiarize myself with this building and present some modicum of ability tomorrow.

The more I walked it the less simple this seemed. At last I decided to walk outside the building to at least find where the main entrance was and where windows were so I could sketch them out. No luck. I was as confused as ever. I would need a helicopter view. No, I did not consider commandeering one of those choppers to get an aerial view, but had I been there a little longer without much more sleep and with less and less sense of good judgment and propriety, that might have been one option considered. Indeed, some weeks later when I was at home watching TV there was a story about two doctors with a hurricane survivor who needed hospitalization and they did just that. They "borrowed" a truck to take their patient for care without wandering through the maze of paperwork, permission slips, and time required by protocol.

Instead I decided to start asking people in the building if they knew where the cafeteria was on the map. Did they know where the bathrooms were on this map; could they show me where the main entrance was on this map? As luck would have it there were many workmen, police, and even some former employees who had worked in this building up until the day before, when it was still the State Farm Insurance Company offices. One person had even been involved in some of the design of the building. Aha, such luck. Of course none of them gave me the same directions, most of them were as perplexed as I was.

I wondered again if this was simply due to sleep deprivation, a pre-Alzheimer's marking, or a general directionally challenged personality disorder. Of course my anxiety level continued to escalate, knowing that I didn't know what I needed to know, and wouldn't know by tomorrow. I must have walked the building for an hour and finally was able to determine where the bathrooms, cafeteria, and cry room were located. The greatest thing was the aerobic benefits to my heart and assistance for weight control this place provided. If Jennie Craig and Weight Watchers could have marketed this technique they would have boosted their quarterly earnings by several points this week. Moving day was tomorrow.

Friday was here. It was the day we were to learn the true meaning of what organized chaos meant. I spent a few short hours at the old shelter. The Monroe Civic Center was bustling with activity as people were packing their things and getting ready to get on busses. Some had their own cars or vans and were getting ready to caravan to the new center. The good thing was that it was only a few short miles away.

The process would take all day. Finally, we were told to go to the new site, the State Farm Building. Busses pulled up outside the building, residents got out and retrieved their belongings from the bus. Of course there were no suitcases to be packed. Residents hand-carried whatever few clothes and belongings they had. Their things were packed in large plastic bags. People lined up to come through the main entrance with their families. Sometimes families had been separated during the move, and then connected with each other again at the new shelter. No matter how well-intentioned and how well-organized the system, this was still extraordinarily anxiety-provoking. I worried especially for the children. I was to observe a worried look on many faces as grandmothers, children, and parents were not always coming through the entrance at the same time. The facility was one more new place with so many unknowns. When would they eat, what would they eat, where would they sleep, where were the bathrooms? Those persons needing medications for heart problems, diabetes, and disabilities—how would they manage these additional needs during this transition? These must have been just some of the questions.

The guards who had worked at the Monroe Civic Center transferred over to the old State Farm Building. As people entered the new building, each was scanned with a wand by the National Guard to be sure there were no weapons brought in. Their bags were put through an X-ray scanning conveyer exactly like the kind that airlines use.

That the process of moving needed to be as simple, speedy, efficient, and as cost effective as possible was easily understandable, yet I could not help but think about those huge black plastic bags going through the conveyer belt. They were garbage bags, the kind we buy at the supermarket to throw our trash into. What kind of lasting impression would that impart to the evacuees? What message would be sent to them about how their possessions were perceived? Were their possessions just so much trash? Were there any subtle messages about how much value these lives held? Would I be the only one to think this way?

At this point during the process a great sadness came over me. It was seemingly out of the blue. I pulled myself off to one side and dissolved into tears. I soon realized that this process reminded me of what my own grandparents and parents must have been experiencing as they escaped Nazi persecution in Europe almost a century ago. My parents and grandparents came to Ellis Island in New York and experienced the fears of not knowing how they would be treated, would they be safe, could they communicate, would they have food, where would they live, would they find jobs. They did not speak the language, and they feared being turned back if anyone was found with a cough or anything that might be considered contagious.

Though I was born in this country many years later, the fears and anxieties of that time were transmitted to my generation and will be carried forward for generations to come. On this day, watching Hurricane Katrina evacuees go through this process, it triggered the memories of stories told by my family and the many untold events I learned only through textbooks in school. The point is that trauma may appear to lie dormant and not be affecting anyone, but it does not go away and in fact will affect future generations. Here, today, it was affecting me almost a hundred years after my family's experience of leaving Europe and arriving in New York City.

I wondered about some of these families, especially the young children. They came through on one end of the line with a relative and had to wait for mothers at the other end. I worried about the families whose husbands, wives, and children were still missing. What effect would this have in the years to come? How would this event in time affect these families and their future generations in the years to come? What would the emotional toll be? I don't believe we, the general American public have a fraction of awareness of the impact this will have in the future.

When we watch someone being saved heroically and physically from a flood, a fire, an earthquake, a plane wreck, we generally think all is well now that they have been saved. As a culture we still do not understand or have sufficient empathy for emotional trauma. We just expect people to "get over it, you are safe now." We still think people are weak when they require mental health counseling.

As a culture we have not come to grips with the importance of good preventive mental health. We go for dental check-ups and we go for medical check-ups. But we are still in the Middle Ages in terms of mental health care. We are so perplexed when we read in the paper about a mother who murders her children, or a teenager who shoots his schoolmates, or an employee who shoots his employer. We seem so clueless and yet the signs have been in these individuals long ago. We simply have closed our eyes and chosen not to put our resources in this arena. We pay a huge price for this omission.

We pay an enormous price internationally with regards to the currently popular topic of terrorism, but that is for another book and for another person to write about. The point here is to ponder the importance of nurturance, stability, and security early on in childhood development and to provide preventive care rather than just reactive care. It is similar to eating a good diet, and getting enough sleep and exercise versus providing surgery to clear arteries of cholesterol build-up or a coronary bypass for a life of poor habits.

While I certainly do not condone it, I can understand why people use drugs, alcohol, and violence to deal with the fears, to block the feelings of pain, to block the feelings of helplessness, and hopelessness. They are cheap and readily available. They are an instant quick fix. Therapy, counseling, real assistance with housing, job development, fair wages, working conditions, education, discrimination—these take time and cost more in the short run. Of course in the long run they are the components that provide the foundation for a healthy society.

As a social worker I advocate for the long-range plan. In general it is the action-packed, quick and dramatic rescues and similar events that sell newspapers, magazines, and TV time. I hope the media will increasingly turn its spotlight on the huge emotional price we pay by not understanding more of the nature of emotional trauma and the ways to mediate it. I hope the media will devote more time and space to delve into the deeper meanings about the underlying causes of acts of violence. What occurrences in childhood cause a young man to develop hatred? Why does a young mother hear voices to kill her children? How does it begin? What can be done to prevent this? The media is powerful and can be used in the vital role of educating.

The Balloon Lady

I'M AT THE new facility. People are coming through the lines, their bags and belongings are being searched. Now what do I do? I'm supposed to be doing orientation, but whatever that meant never did become clear to me. I decide to position myself at the other end of the conveyer belt, and then I am quickly relieved to learn there are many volunteers who will guide, direct, and walk with families to their cots to deliver their belongings. There are many wonderful volunteers who are helping to carry belongings on carts and by hand. I have no idea why I did not understand this fully before, but I am so relieved right now. I knew there would be others to help, but it was never clear exactly what they would be doing or how many volunteers would be assisting. I have a strong desire to make sure these evacuees are as comfortable as possible, so this was an enormous relief.

Soon Debbie suggests it might be best to be positioned outside the entrance where there are many people just arriving and getting off the busses. They are standing outside in the sun and the line is moving slowly. It can easily be a half hour or more of waiting in line. As I stand outside and "work the crowd" it is clear there is some tension. Children are children. They want to run and play, and they are tired of waiting, yet they cannot go off to play. Luckily I had filled the many pockets of my Red Cross jacket with balloons and whatever little toys I could find. I still tried sneaking a few cereal bars into any unsuspecting children who had not yet met me.

The tiny toys were fine for a while. Steve and I bought some little wooden toy animals with bobbing heads for some unknown reason in our travels to Mexico and years later still had no idea what to do with them. I had stuffed them in my bag thinking it would be a good way to get the clutter out of our garage, and hoping they might be of some use on this trip. As I walked up and down the line outside, I gave the toys to some of the children. The children loved them. They began comparing them with each other, placing them on the sidewalks and grass, moving their little bobbing heads and tails. It worked . . . for about ten minutes. Then they started coming to me because the heads broke. Quality control was not something the street vendors in Mexico had a huge investment in when we purchased these little turtles and dogs with bobbing heads some years ago. The next best thing to giving refunds was to blow up a few balloons and make faces on them with a marking pen. For a short time this distracted the children. I hoped the line would move more quickly. Looking back on it now I should have bought a gross of balloons to keep in my pockets and would have done so if I had realized how entertaining such a simple item could be. Alas, the cereal bars never did make it to the top ten on a popularity chart. Lollipops were still a hit and I expect the dental profession in Monroe might do very well financially in the months to come.

What Are You Going to Do to Celebrate?

THE NEXT EXPERIENCE was one that I will remember for the rest of my life. It was to be one of the most moving experiences of all the times spent with the Red Cross in this disaster. It was early to mid afternoon, and I went back inside the facility to see what else might be done. A heavy-set grandmother had just come through the line, had her possessions X-rayed and was standing with about three young grandchildren ages four through twelve. She appeared very tired to me, and I surmised she would be more comfortable with a chair. Pulling a chair from another area, I motioned to her and asked if she would like to sit. She was grateful for the small gesture. She was trying to keep her eye on all the children as well as their few possessions of clothing and sheets, and she was waiting for her daughter to arrive. Her daughter had been separated from them and was still outside somewhere, either on a bus or in line waiting to enter the shelter. I gave the children my stash of balloons and again this seemed to keep them temporarily distracted.

One of her grandchildren had been given a small live turtle in a glass bowl of water. I do not know how she got this but it was a wonderful small way to foster learning to care for something else and being able to focus on something fun in this unsettling time. I did not have time to inquire about what the turtle ate but did wonder about it much later. Pets can be a marvelous way to learn about nurturance even in a time of such chaos.

I stayed with this grandmother and we talked for a short time. She was trying so hard to care for her granddaughters and seemed very troubled. She was very protective of the girls and kept them within sight the whole time. We probably spent no more than fifteen minutes together near the entrance, waiting for her daughter to come inside. As we talked she said she had not seen her husband in two weeks and did not know if he got out alive. She was beginning to come to grips with the fact that he was probably dead. She was calm and had given this some thought; she obviously had prepared herself for this inevitability. I turned and walked a few feet away.

I do not know exactly how the next event reached her, but a moment later someone spoke with her and told her that her husband was alive. We were just a few feet apart, and we glanced at each other across the space, instinctively grabbed onto each other, and cried together. We had known each other only for a few moments. I do not recall her name, but the emotions were intense as we shared this moment. It felt as if she were my family. The feelings of loss, of loneliness, fear, relief, and joy are universal. Did I mention we were of different races, ages, religions, and cultural experiences? The shared common emotions bridged any differences and made them irrelevant. We had a momentary bond that was powerful. I wondered about the remote chance that had brought me together with her to share in this moment.

To top this off, a few moments later out of the corner of my eye I saw her walk to a door to join a man who had just arrived. It was her husband.

I never did find out how he came to arrive here and find her in this crowd. They went outside and I could not resist wanting to see them together. I went out to be with her, wanting a few more moments of this time. A TV camera crew began filming. She was still overcome and did not want to face them or talk. It was her husband who did the talking. With my arm on her shoulder she finally turned and briefly spoke with the reporter.

I thought for a moment and asked her husband if he had any plans to celebrate. He had not yet given it a thought. In my still simplistic, silly way I reached into a pocket and found a pink balloon, which of course I blew up and handed to him. That was the last I saw of them. There was no time to watch TV that night, and I do not even recall clearly which station filmed this event although I vaguely recall seeing some X's on a camera, perhaps as in Fox TV. I never got to see this moment on TV, but it is one of my treasured memories of this event.

Pizza Delivery

Soon after this, on Saturday, our mental health unit met to determine schedules for the rest of the week. We were to staff twenty-four hours a day. Some of us would have to work the evening shift of 10:00 p.m. to 6:00 a.m. These are not exactly the coveted schedules one relishes. My colleague Susan and I decided that since we were the seasoned veterans (being here for five days) it would be helpful for the new volunteers if we took the evening shift. We knew many of the residents and the general mode of operating. New volunteers would be arriving shortly and they would be better off working during the day when they would have a full staff to work with and they could more easily become familiar with the setting.

We had already worked most of the morning shift that day (from 7:00 a.m. to 2:00 p.m.), so we went back to the motel where we were staying. Susan was much wiser than I. She had been on many disasters before and she went to sleep to prepare for the evening shift. I naively did not do so. I read, made some phone calls back home, did some note taking and generally collected my thoughts. I decided that I probably would not be needed much longer since there would be three new mental health volunteers arriving the next day. I would have been due to have a day off after nine days anyway and considered making plans to leave sometime the next day.

Saturday night was the last night I worked at the shelter. Susan and I arrived at 10:00 p.m., and it felt strange. Of course it was lightly staffed and most people were asleep in their cots. Still, many people were awake, and some were milling about. We each walked around separately, continuing to pick up the tenor of the place and determine what was needed. In general, I was pleased again to note things seemed very calm. No doubt everyone was exhausted from the day's move, and therefore any discontent and fear would probably be on vacation for at least this night.

Over the past few days while we'd worked at the civic center, food had been brought in during the regular dinner hour. This, however, was late evening and there was no formal dinner, just a few snacks. But, once again, it continued to be another wonderful experience at this new shelter. A local restaurant delivered what seemed like hundreds of pizzas for the volunteers. The community continued to pour out its heart and generosity. The police, the National Guard, the nurses, and whoever the volunteers were on the late shift that night all shared in the very welcome food.

I began to walk the facility to visit with residents and came upon Mary, the young mother who had previously been having trouble with managing her young toddler, John. It must have been around midnight, but John was still awake because he was thirsty and hungry. Mary could not sleep while he was still awake. In our previous shelter, the Monroe Civic Center, snacks had been always available, but there was more formality here. The cafeteria locked its doors in the evening, and there was not yet a plan in place for providing food in the late evening. I was able to find some juice for John and some form of sugary snack to satisfy him. After talking with Mary it was learned that she had not had any dinner that night. Of course the solution was to go back to the volunteer station, siphon off a pizza, and deliver it to Mary in bed. She was most appreciative.

It appeared Mary had gained some new awareness of what was normal for John going through this hectic time. She seemed to be more patient with him. I passed her bed again about an hour later and noted John had gone to sleep in one corner of a large mattress, and Mary was asleep next to him. It was the last time I saw Mary.

Though I would have liked to say a more formal goodbye, I was not yet fully certain at this point that I would be leaving the next day. This remains a bit of a loose end for me. I have come to understand that all does not go smoothly in a crisis and all of my needs for completion could not be taken care of. I take comfort in the thought that Mary could put John in the wonderful day care center which was on site at that shelter. I knew she could join one of the parent groups to learn more about child development and that she would have an opportunity to share her experiences with other young mothers. She could join a group lead by local volunteer community mental health social workers and psychologists. I did not get to see if those connections were made but I trust that Mary was assertive enough to seek them out, and that she learned to trust the Red Cross volunteers. I feel so uplifted to know these wonderful services were available. And I know if my current career does not work out I could deliver pizzas back in California.

The Baby Needs to Eat

I WENT BACK to doing rounds. It was probably 1:00 a.m. or so. A young mother was standing next to her cot with a newborn infant of about one month old. She was struggling in the dark with a bottle, adding powdered formula. She added bottled water and shook the bottle. I stopped to talk with her and learned that she needed someplace to heat the bottle. There were microwaves in the cafeteria, and by this time I hoped I would be able to find my way there even in the dark. I thought about taking the bottle to the cafeteria, heating it and returning it to her, but given my still dubious sense of direction, I had visions of never ever finding mother and baby again in the dark. I asked her to follow me with the baby. She sleepily but willingly followed.

When we got there, we found the cafeteria doors were locked. The guard in the hall said they were not due to open again until morning, and he did not have the key or the authority to open them. By now I reasoned it was time to find his supervisor and asked him to do so. A few minutes later a very tall National Guardsman arrived. He walked with a certain sense of authority. I did not know his rank, but he clearly presented himself as someone in charge. I told him of the need to use a microwave to heat the bottle. At first his look was one which concerned me. He sighed and reiterated the rule that no one was to enter the cafeteria during the night. My expectation of the military is that generally they are very good at following rules. This was going to take some finesse.

I stepped back so that the young mother with her new infant would be about two feet in front of him and directly in his line of sight. He looked at her, seemed to take a long look and suddenly declared, "Well, the baby needs to eat." He went about getting the keys to unlock the cafeteria. I wondered when he looked at her if he himself did not have a young child at home, but I was not going to take this time to engage him in conversation. I was just happy he chose to change the situation.

I went with the mother into the cafeteria, turned on the lights, and found a microwave to heat the bottle. She heated the bottle and we walked back together to her bed. This was not one of the most fascinating events of this time. We didn't have any long conversations, but it was one more time when I could feel the merits of having been there to work the night shift. Had someone not been there for her, I'm not sure she would have had the energy to get up and look for someone to help her. It is just one example of what life in a shelter was like during this time.

One Last Goodbye

ON THIS LAST night there was a chance to meet a few of the residents whom I had not met before. It was an opportunity to listen to more stories, to connect and be of whatever comfort possible. One such contact was with a young, very attractive, trim blond woman of about twenty-five or so. She was wearing one of those scrub-type outfits that nurses wear, and I mistakenly thought she was a Red Cross nurse. She was well-groomed and sitting in the staff area late at night. It was not until talking with her for a while that I realized she was a survivor of Hurricane Katrina and not a nurse. She had gotten the scrub outfit from the used clothing choices at the shelter. She talked of the difficulties in getting out of New Orleans and I listened, as usual.

At some point during this listening it occurred to me that we at the Red Cross are generally trained to listen to stories over and over again so that people can feel some sense of catharsis. While recognizing that this is an important part of the healing, I still wanted to see more of the hopefulness for the future. I wanted to see it more quickly than is generally thought of as appropriate for crisis counseling. I wanted to position this young woman to begin to look at the future and gather what she had learned. I wanted to plant seeds for how to go forward and to think about strengths she possessed. Some questions popped up in my mind and I asked her, "Did anything positive come out of this for you? . . . And is there anything you will do differently as you go forward?" It was a marvelous experience for me as I asked these questions.

This particular young woman said she had learned to be more independent, to do more things for herself and not depend on her father to do everything for her. Although she was in her twenties she had never written a check. Her father still wrote all her checks for her. She said she was not going to allow that to be done any more. She had a fairly healthy sense of herself. She held some bottom-level clerical position and was planning to find a similar job and go back to work. We talked about her experience and she indicated she had two years of college, yet she did not even consider returning to college and had no money to do so. It was evident that she was bright, verbal, and could be more assertive and look for better opportunities in the future. I asked her if she ever considered applying for a scholarship or getting a loan. We talked about opportunities she had not considered. This was only a beginning and I hope that some seeds were planted and she will carry the thoughts through into her future.

Later on, about 3:00 a.m. on this last night working at the new shelter, I was walking around, checking the beds and halls to see if all was okay. In the main hall, near the entrance, I saw Linda, the woman who had been depressed about her dogs and had screamed one day back at the Monroe Civic Center. She was sitting with her boyfriend, Mitchell. They had their bags with them and were waiting for a ride to the airport. Her sister had been able to get enough money for a plane ticket for both of them, and they would soon be leaving.

I sat with them for a few minutes and we reviewed how things were going. I then asked them the same questions, had anything good come of this, and was there anything they would do differently in their new lives. Mitchell said yes, for sure. He started to talk and admitted he had been dabbling with either alcohol and/or drugs in the past and was at this moment wanting to talk about it. He had a dubious work history and had been living with Linda for several years, unwilling to make any long-term commitment to the relationship. He said he was not going to do that again, and he had a new view of what was important in life. He needed to get serious about life. He said they would be getting married.

His words were so simple, yet so profound, and are memorable to me today. He simply said **"I realize I don't have forever."**

Linda said, "Thank you for everything." I said I didn't do anything, just sat with her and listened. We gave each other a big hug as she was leaving and she said, "Oh yes, you did. You made a big difference to me." I am still amazed and touched by how simple it all is—to just hug, to listen, and to be there. I am still amazed that these simple gestures can be so intense in the moment. I am still amazed that weeks and even months later whenever I recall this time tears often stream down my face. There is a sadness that I will never see Linda or Mike again, and a sadness that I did not let them know how much they touched my life too.

Chapter 8

Random Acts of Kindness

DURING OUR STAY in Louisiana one early evening Sue and I needed to get dinner before working the evening shift. We were of course tired, and had not changed out of our Red Cross jackets as we headed for the first place within walking distance of our motel. It was a small, simple, and modestly priced Italian restaurant. The food was very basic and the restaurant was busy. We were served in a reasonable amount of time by a pleasant waitress, and there was nothing memorable about the service or the menu. The only thing I do recall about the very few times when we ate out was the importance of always taking back what we did not eat. At home I often do this when in a restaurant, but not to the degree that happened here. At home I would usually take back food only if there was something I really wanted. Now it was the rolls, the baked potato, anything that someone back at the shelter might want. The impressions of loss and deprivation were incredibly imprinted on me and the thought of waste was intolerable.

On this day it seemed to take forever for our waitress to return with our check. I surmised she was busy, had forgotten about us, and went to look for her. Finally, I determined it was best to go to the kitchen to look for her or we would be here forever. Finding her and asking about our bill she said, "Oh your bill has been paid." She explained that a couple sitting at a table in the corner had paid our bill. They were no longer in the restaurant. I do not know if they were young, old, what race they were, or anything about them. They did not wait for a thank you. This beautiful, simple gesture was one of the many ways that Louisiana said thank you to us. It was one more of the gestures that I will remember forever. It was one more experience of how tragedy can lead some to reach out with selfless acts of kindness, with no expectation of even a thank-you.

Again and again throughout this time in Louisiana there were total strangers, people who stopped on the street, while at work, while boarding a plane, to reach over and to simply say, "Thank you for coming." They were such genuine expressions of appreciation and they were so welcome.

Chapter 9

The Road Less Traveled:
Southern Hospitality

AFTER THIS LAST night in the shelter it was clear I did not really need to stay. There were many others to take my place. Yes, there were still many needs; yes, I had formed bonds and relationships with many of the people; and yes, I could still be of help. However, Steve was at home, there was a job to go back to, children to talk with again, and neighbors I wanted to get back to. I did not want to be one of those who thought no one else could do the job without them. I was relieved to know there would be three other volunteers coming tomorrow . . . Gee, did it take three people to do what I had done? Seriously, it was a natural time to go and great that it would happen after having so many positive experiences.

Sue had been wonderful and was willing to give up the car and let me drive it back to Baton Rouge for a flight the next day. We found a new motel for her to stay in that was within walking distance of the shelter. It would be easier for her, and she did not need the hassle of driving.

Up until this time Sue had done all the driving. She had the entire responsibility. She was happy to do the driving, and I was happy to let her, but it was now my responsibility to drive back to Baton Rouge in preparation to leave for California. I was determined to not get lost.

After saying some goodbyes to the volunteers I surmised that my best
bet was to ask some of the local police which the best roads were. Armed
with my yellow highlighter and a state map, brought from home, I dou-
ble-checked with no less than two local police officers, who were staffing
the center, and one volunteer, who lived in Monroe. All assured me that
the shorter and better route was not the major highway that Sue and I
had driven on our way up. With a new sense of directional confidence
I said goodbye to Sue and proceeded on my way. I was determined to
stop and verify directions all along the way, before becoming unsure,
and this was to serve me very well. I did not get lost even once on the
trip back, and for me this was another accomplishment.

The road back proved to be far more interesting than the main highway. It passed through small towns. Many cotton fields and cotton mills
were to be seen along the way. Small town life and the real deep Southern
culture were more evident now than on the road we originally took. I en-
joyed being able to take this all in with a relatively slow pace. The shelter
experience had been so rapid and so intense that this was now a welcome
bit of time alone. There was no one to be responsible for. No laundry to
do, no house to clean, no meals to cook, no reports to write. It was the
first really calm period in almost ten days and it was relished.

The trip took longer than expected. What was billed initially as two
to three hours turned out to be more like a five-hour venture. True, I
did stop several times for a break, for gas, and for something to eat, and
plus I did have one unplanned exposure to Southern hospitality.

Somewhere along this leisurely drive it began getting dark and I realized I still had a distance to go. It was a quiet road with barely any other
cars passing on the road . . . and then there was clearly a car behind me
with the all-too-familiar and unwelcome sound of a siren. Yes, it was
the police. I pulled over to the side and rolled down the window as a
Louisiana patrolman came to the side of the car. Of course I had been
going too fast.

Yup, "You were going fifty-four miles an hour, lady. This is a forty-five mile an hour zone," he said. I apologized meekly, saying I was sorry and had been a bit stressed in trying to get back home. He seemed unimpressed as he looked at me. He took a longer hard glance at me and I became a bit concerned. This was a quiet road, no one passing, starting to get dark, and I was alone. I tried to explain I was unfamiliar with this part of the country and was heading back home to California after a long week here in Louisiana. He took a longer look and slowly looked all over the car. Finally he said, "Are you with the Red Cross?" He had noted the shirt I was wearing and the Red Cross sticker in the back side window. "Take it easy, lady—there's a small town ahead and the speed limit there is thirty-five," he said as he walked off. My instinct was to hug him, but my common sense ruled and I gratefully drove off, this time staying very carefully within the speed limit. This was one experience with Southern hospitality that I was not eager to repeat.

Chapter 10

When Do I Get Off Work?

SOMEWHERE ALONG THE drive I needed to stop for a break. There were very few stores, it was getting dark, and when I found a location I eagerly pulled in to rest for a few minutes. Realizing I would need to recoup some energy I decided to walk around a bit and went into the store to look around. This was the closest to recreational shopping I would have in Louisiana. This store was a mini-micro-discount-type store or a slightly large convenience store with a little bit of everything. I found some cheap reading glasses for $5, which I decided to buy to boost the local economy.

It was late Saturday night, and the store was just closing. The clerk at the register was a young woman who could not have been more than eighteen. She was clearly eager to be out of there as quickly as possible. She needed a price for an item and literally screamed an ear-piercing scream across the floor to someone to get her a price for an item. She apparently did not have training in customer service as she repeatedly screamed several times rather than use the microphone or telephone which was in clear view next to the register.

As I waited in line to pay for the glasses there were two mothers in front of me with three young children. They all looked tired and were running out of patience as they waited for the clerk to get a price check.

One of the little girls, about five years old, was irritable and beginning to cry. Her mother was out of patience, was yelling at her, and then began smacking her. In California no doubt someone would have been looking over her shoulder and considering calling the county Child Protective Services. Here in this part of Louisiana, on Saturday night, with only a young clerk eager to be off work, it appeared this was completely within the norm of what was understandable and acceptable child care.

Luckily there were still some balloons left in a pocket of the Red Cross jacket that I was still wearing. By this time I was on automatic pilot and began blowing one up and asking her mother if it was okay to give her daughter one. It was fine with her mother, and it worked. For the moment there was some quiet in the store and the mom had a brief break. The bigger problem was that the two other children now wanted balloons too, and they might be fussy over which colors they wanted. Fortunately, there were a few more balloons left in the same pocket and the children were all easily engaged in deciding on colors. Thinking about it now I wonder if a balloon would have kept the darn clerk more socially sophisticated and more tolerable. Can't I realize I'm not still volunteering at the shelter? Am I not off work? Why do I need to do this? Will I continue to give coworkers, my husband, my supervisor, a balloon when things are tense?

Chapter 11

What's in a Name?

I WAS STILL DRIVING, and was now within an hour of Baton Rouge. It was soon time to stop for something to eat. It was now totally dark and the thought of finding healthy California-style veggies or gourmet dining was not even a remote consideration. It would indeed be fortunate to find something open. The choice came down to three places, all fairly close to each other. The first one had a long wait and specialized in hamburgers. The second one was closing in a few minutes and specialized in hamburgers. The third one…could you guess? It was McDonald's. One definitely must pack a sense of humor to volunteer for any such ventures. The only other possibility was to request admission to a nearby psychiatric facility and hope they serve more than hamburgers.

McDonald's it was! Upon entering, I saw a typed message on the door indicating that a local clothing store was accepting clothing donations for the refugees of Hurricane Katrina. Indeed, it was almost impossible to go to any corner of any town in Louisiana without finding some sign for donations and a request for help. There were requests for collections of food and offers of shelter or meals in so many places. The word on the sign said **refugees** and that word stood out. The night before, my last night working in the shelter, I sat near a man who was watching TV by himself into the early morning hours. It must have been about 3:00 or 4:00 a.m., and I sat with him to watch for a few minutes. He was cold and had few clothes with him. He did have a blanket, which I kept pulling over his shoulders. We didn't talk much, we just sat together. The newscaster was talking about New Orleans and the refugees. The man snickered and said "refugees" in a disdainful and questioning manner. He objected to the use of this term. "Refugees are people from another country, but we live right here."

I entered McDonald's thinking of this man and what he had said. I looked at the menu, trying to find something healthful. Feeling very proud of myself, I ordered the apple and walnut salad. Gee, was I really able to do this? Maybe I've turned a corner and can live on good food anywhere. Did I really pass up a Big Mac with fries and a shake? After all no one would even see me eat this stuff. And didn't I deserve to treat myself to something delicious and filling after this long week and this long trip? Once again, a great smug feeling of having outsmarted the food industry came over me. It was actually great. I didn't need to clog any more arteries or help improve the bottom line for any cardiologists. These apples were just sweet enough to soothe, and the crunching on the walnuts satisfied any lingering biting anger.

The sign in the door still had me thinking about the term evacuee. Why can't I just leave it alone? In my former life I was a teacher. Do I need to continue to fill the role of educator right now? Of course not . . . So why do I feel compelled to speak with the manager? Who cares why? I found myself asking to speak with the manager and indicating that the sign on the front door, while in a very good spirit, was still not accurate in its terminology. I explained that these folks from New Orleans were neighbors and not from another country and some of them were upset with not being thought of as neighbors. The correct term was evacuee. She listened patiently and said the sign was not hers. It was written by the local clothing store. The owners of that store would not be back again or open until Monday. It was typed on a computer and she could not change it. Oh well . . . I had tried.

We talked a bit about New Orleans, whether she had any relatives there, and whether they were all okay. She said all her family was safe but one of her employees had an aunt who still was unaccounted for. A few minutes later she walked to the door, took the sign down, scratched out the word refugee and hand-wrote evacuee in place of the word refugee. She came back to the table where I was sitting and said, "At least I know how to spell evacuee." Then, as she taped the sign back up, she said, "They probably couldn't spell it, anyway," referring to the owners of the clothing store.

Chapter 12

The Bulletproof Vest

LATE THAT NIGHT I arrived in Baton Rouge and headed for the last shelter I was assigned to sleep in. On the way there it was time to get gas. The part of town where this shelter was located was away from the town center, and gas was getting low. I decided to stop wherever a station was open. The week before, while living in Baton Rouge, there had been a gas shortage. People were waiting in line for up to an hour to get gas. In fact, many stations had been sold out of gas on some days and it was necessary to wait until the next day. I was not going to take any chances with an empty tank at night. When I spotted a station ahead I pulled in and started to pump gas. Getting ready to pay, I put the credit card into the slot on the pump, but a message flashed saying, "Please go inside to see the attendant."

As I looked around I could see lots of young men hanging out on one side of the front door of the store. Most of them seemed to be in their late teens. All of them had their pants hanging down in the current fashion. One of them had pants hanging so low he had to walk with one hand holding them up. It was more a fashion show of bright underwear than anything else. If this were daytime, if this were a well-populated part of town, if it were my hometown and I felt familiar and comfortable here, it would have been comical. Instead, in this time and place it began to concern me.

To the other side of the door were several older men, one of whom had a brown paper bag with something inside that he was sipping from, and I didn't think it was hot cocoa. This was Saturday night in a part of town that did not look particularly prosperous. There were no women in sight except for the cashier, who was sitting behind one of those thick Plexiglas kind of booths I've seen in a local bank at home. I believe we refer to them as bulletproof shields in California. It was clear that the entertainment aspect of this part of town involved drinking and hanging around on the corner with not much to do. It was definitely not where or how I would have chosen to spend a free Saturday evening alone.

Strategy was clear. I needed gas. I needed to pay for it, and I needed to stay safe. I reached back into the backseat, pulled on my trusty Red Cross vest with the words **Red Cross Disaster** written in huge, bold, reflective letters on the back. I was not going to chance having these young and restless adolescents miss seeing the tiny emblem on my dark red shirt in the dark at night.

Pulling the car up directly in front of the entrance, I raced for the door, paid for the gas, and attempted to run back outside. As could have been expected, one of the older gentlemen, the one with the paper bag and bottle, teetered over to me to engage in conversation. He was clearly a bit wobbly on his feet, as well as taller and obviously stronger than I. This was not my turf, so I decided to be as polite as possible till he could get out of my way. We probably spent all of three minutes talking about the flood and I inquired if all his friends and family were okay. It turned out that he really wanted to be very helpful and be sure I had the right directions to where I was going. It was one more of those experiences that turned out well, thanks to the good old Red Cross attire. In fact, it was directly after this event that I toyed with the idea of never taking this vest off. It literally felt like I had a bulletproof vest on.

Chapter 13

Pack Light: Start with Two Bags, Return with One

THE LAST NIGHT was spent sleeping in a small shelter that had been set up very late that night. It was the sparsest of any of the shelters I had been to. This was a recreation center, not a church. There were no showers. The great part was that it was small and I was able to connect briefly with a few of the volunteers who were all very congenial, as were most volunteers. As it turned out the shelter manager was the only volunteer I met from New York, and his name was Steve. How could I not connect? My husband, Steve, and I both lived in New York before getting married and during our first two years of marriage. This Steve was retired and my Steve and I have been talking about retiring. It was a welcome connection to end on and I felt some sadness upon leaving a new friend that next morning. Although this recreation center was far out of the way of the rest of the town, I felt totally safe and cared for there.

Once again I was unable to sleep for very long and got up about 2:00 a.m. to do some exercise right outside the front door. A car began circling and a young couple drove over and got out. They were new volunteers and had experienced trouble finding this place. They had been driving all night and were exhausted. They had never been to a shelter and did not know what to expect. It was clear they wanted to help but were unprepared for the lack of comfort and lack of privacy. Steve found a spot for them to sleep in that was outside the main room so they would not be awakened when everyone else awakened soon. They definitely needed sleep, but they were worried about not being able to be ready for the next morning. Steve assured them it would be okay to get to the Red Cross office late the next day. "You are useless without sleep anyway," he said. At this point I was most happy to give them my pillow, sheets, sleeping mat, and anything else I had that they could use. It would be so much easier for me not to lug these things back on the plane, and this young couple could donate them to a shelter when they went home if they wanted to. They both seemed happy to have these few items and they quickly went to sleep. As I got ready to leave the shelter this last morning I had one balloon left in a pocket. I blew it up, wrote "Good Morning" on it with a marking pen, and then wrapped it in a towel they would use near their cot in the morning. I hoped it would humor and cheer them up when they woke.

On the last leg of this trip I arrived early at the chapter office ready to check out and finish all the paperwork needed before leaving. People were starting to line up early to go get information about FEMA. One family stopped me to ask some FEMA questions, all of which I knew nothing about. They were particularly upset about not getting services and having lost all their possessions. As with so many others they had only the clothing they were wearing and they were looking for clothes. They were definitely angry. We talked for a few minutes and I indicated I was leaving to go back home, but there would be others to help inside. Returning to the car to clear out the trunk before going to the airport there was now one empty duffle bag that I'd previously stuffed with my pillow, sheets, and other linens. Here was one more thing I could happily live without. I brought it to the family, indicating they were sure to get clothing soon and asked if they could use this in the future. The anger was somewhat dissipated, in at least one of the women who said thank you for the gesture.

Leaving to come to Louisiana there were two cases packed. Going home was so much easier. I was very happy to have only a backpack now to juggle on the plane. No curling irons, hair dryers, or mascara to be accounted for. I'd had no makeup of any kind for the entire time there. I absolutely looked like the biggest schlep but felt as if I had won the lottery a million times over.

Chapter 14

Show Me the Money!

Arriving home, Steve met me at the airport and it was great to be back. He asked if he could carry my bags and proceeded to walk toward baggage arrival. I delightedly said "This is it!" as I came off the plane and pointed to the backpack on my back. Steve offered to take me out for dinner and asked where I wanted to go. It was incredibly strange. I'm always happy to eat out. It has been one of those recreational events I lived for. The oddest thing was that I could not decide where I wanted to go or what I wanted to eat. Finally, I just said, "Let's go to my favorite place, the Whole Foods grocery store," where I often go for lunch.

As we arrived at Whole Foods, I experienced an overwhelming feeling of sadness. We looked at the rows and rows of abundant food in the counters, so beautifully prepared, but I could not choose a food. An unexplainable feeling of melancholy came over me, and I found myself unable to eat. The image of people who did not have such choices, who did not have food, who were happy to have a cold pizza delivery in the middle of the night, or a saved baked potato from my dinner one night, were somehow with me, and I could not eat. At that moment it was not possible to enjoy food, knowing and seeing what I had just seen. I found myself pulling off to one side and once again dissolving into tears. For a while I wondered if I would enjoy food ever again. It was not a good feeling.

The next morning Steve had an early morning Rotary meeting. He had joined a new committee while I was gone, which was just set up to raise money for Hurricane Katrina survivors. I wanted very much to go to meet them and say thank you for the work they were doing. It was wonderful to meet these community business leaders who were taking time out of their other commitments to help with this disaster. Over the next few weeks they would raise $50,000. They were considering partnering with other clubs to help plan to rebuild Louisiana, and since then they have raised well in excess of $100,000.

The next day I went back to work at San Andreas Regional Center. It is a nonprofit agency, and we work to serve those with developmental disabilities. We are case managers, social workers, psychologists, clerical staff, fiscal staff, and management. None of us are highly paid. I was hoping the agency might have collected a few hundred dollars. During those ten days while I was gone my coworkers had raised over $4,000 for the Red Cross and other agencies. Tierney hand-delivered a check to the local Red Cross Santa Clara chapter. At my desk the e-mails took two days to get through. Everyone wanted to stop and talk. It was impossible to get any work done. I decided to put together a slide show and talk with my coworkers over lunch about the experience or I would never get any agency work done. There is great pride in working with such generous and wonderful coworkers.

It was a great experience to be able to be in Louisiana and have direct contact with the people and the community. To be able to see, feel, hear, touch, and taste what had occurred was such a privilege. I feel especially fortunate to have been able to have this experience and have the freedom to be able to go to the South at this time. There were so many others who would have liked to go but could not because of family concerns, health issues, or work constraints. It is only with the help of the people back home and around the country who raised money that we are able to do this work, and I am so appreciative of those efforts.

Chapter 15

Reflections: Why Did Some
Turn to Violence?

BEING HOME NOW for several weeks there has been time to think again and again about how some of the people got through these events. Some were angry, some were bitter, some were seriously mentally ill. By far, however, most were appreciative and wanted to move on with their lives. All had lost their possessions; some had lost family members and friends. All were facing great unknowns. With all the possible comforts and amenities provided at the shelters I met only one man who was happy and wanted to stay there. He was a local town drunk who came in to spend a night there, which we allowed. I spent half an hour finding him a cot, blankets, sheets and a place to set his cot up. An hour later I discovered he was still not in his cot. He was sitting near the staff and clearly just wanted something to eat and to be with people for a while.

What was it that made the differences between those who were bitter and mentally ill, and those who were still relatively stable? I've wondered this often as I work in the field of social work. Why do some people do well and others not do well when they are facing the same hardships? People live in poverty, with disabilities, and with physical ailments, and still some do well and others don't. People live in wealth and privilege, and some do well and others don't. What is it? Is there one thing?

If I could answer that question definitively it would be at least a book unto itself. I would like to take this opportunity to reflect on what I have seen in Louisiana and what was so crystal clear to me. It mirrors my experience of years of work in the field of social work. On one level it seems so simple. Those who did well had friends, family, and connections. They were supported and involved in life. No matter how dysfunctional their family systems were, there was still a family there. Even the town drunk that came in saying he wanted a bed and food really didn't go to sleep. He spent his time into the wee hours of the morning talking with the staff and being with people. There was still contact, no matter how negative; there was still a connection.

Those who did the most poorly, the ones with serious mental illness, did not have connections. It didn't seem to matter much to most people if they were fed, clothed, housed, or whether they were alive or dead. These were the folks who babbled on and on to themselves, rocked in their chairs, did not want to be near others, accused others of being deceitful, and so on, and no one really wanted to be with them either. The clearest observation was the lack of social connections.

Chapter 16

How Can We Protect Ourselves?

THOSE OF US who have been lucky enough to never experience a major disaster sometimes are lulled into the belief it cannot happen to us. We think it will not happen in the United States. We are educated, have a strong democratic government, and many of us think nothing will ever go wrong. If something does go wrong we think that somehow we will be taken care of. Those of us who live in California on the San Andreas Fault are incredibly naïve and consciously think it will never happen here. I certainly hope not in my lifetime, my children's lifetimes, my potential grandchildren's lifetimes, and so on. I, you, and we are living in what is called a state of denial.

Many of us have read newspaper articles, watched TV programs, and obtained lists of items to keep at home, at work, and in cars to prepare for any eventual disasters. Those of us who live in California are frequently reminded of the need to be prepared. Our local hardware stores and supermarkets often have displays of flashlights, batteries, radios, and water prominently displayed at entrances whenever there is an impending disaster, local storm expected, or one that has just occurred. Stores often sell prepared kits and backpacks with tools and medical kits containing bandages, antiseptic ointments, and so forth. Our own health care provider sold such kits years ago. The Red Cross sells such kits. There are numerous resources and classes for CPR and first-aid that are offered. I have taken such classes, purchased these supplies, given one to my husband, and sent one to each of my children. We each have them in our cars. At least I hope so—I did send you each one years ago, Steve, David, and Michelle!

These are all excellent resources and I would urge everyone to be prepared with supplies and training. The truth is that during this experience with people in Louisiana I learned that many of the people had these supplies; many of them were well-trained and knew how to be as independent as possible. Yet when the floods came all these well-planned-out supplies were lost. For those of us in an earthquake zone it is clear there is not much time to access things, no matter how well-prepared we may be.

In the weeks following Katrina we have witnessed over and over again disasters throughout the world. Floods and mudslides have destroyed thousands of lives. We have seen how the magnitude of these conditions can overcome even the most powerful among us.

As I reflected back about what happened in Louisiana, about the people who did well and those who did not, it occurred to me that there was one thing not on the list of things to stockpile. That thing was people. That thing was relationships. That thing was family and connections. We do not shop for this in a store and have it in a day. It is a continual process of working at it over the years of our lives.

If you have young children and only a flashlight when a storm occurs, that is not enough. Do you know a neighbor well enough to knock on the door to ask for food, could you ask for medical help if you needed it, do you know a neighbor's name, do you have a relative to contact? Could you go next door or walk your neighborhood to ask who might need help?

In our neighborhood there are several families fortunate enough to have swimming pools. They could easily supply the entire neighborhood for weeks with safe chlorinated water if need be, but this works only if we know each other. In our neighborhood we are fortunate to have a young fireman living nearby who knows CPR. We have friends who know first-aid. How much easier will it be if we know each other before we have such needs?

The thing we most need to stockpile is relationships. It is my hope if you had the patience to read this far in the book you will seriously give this consideration, introduce yourself to someone new, hug a new body, and continue to stockpile relationships.

Chapter 17

So How Was Your Vacation?

I **DIDN'T KNOW IT** in the beginning, but this would turn out to be one of the most positive, inspirational, uplifting experiences of my sixty-four years. It was a privilege to be able to be so close and feel so connected to those living in the shelters, those who were grappling with and trying to resolve how to rebuild their lives. I am so fortunate to have been allowed into this world to see, taste, touch, and smell this time in history. There was little room for artificiality. There was little energy to hold back much emotion. There was little room for intolerance or discrimination. The energy was needed to figure out how to survive and move forward. We were there to hug and hold, to comfort, to feed, to make plans, and to just be with the tears.

So what is a vacation? Is it not a time for change, for renewal, and for rejuvenation? When I came back my arthritis was almost gone. I was able to close my left hand early in the morning without difficulty…and I was almost five pounds lighter.

The experience was overwhelming. Of course being up day and night, exercising each day, walking the halls of an eight-acre shelter containing almost 1,000 people, sometimes working twelve and more hours a day, and generally not eating junk food, did play a role. Now where is that purple dress?

Afterword

THERE WERE COUNTLESS examples of how our skills as social workers and psychologists were put to the test. I have chosen just a few examples to write about in the hope that they will inspire others to volunteer in the future and fill the Red Cross with many excellent mental health and other workers. There is such a vital need and this work was incredibly rewarding. I think this adrenalin rush must be similar to what it must feel like to be on drugs. In the moment it is very intense. I could not do it forever and it takes time to recuperate, but it has lasted many weeks and months and I would do it again in a heartbeat.

About the Author

ANNETTE LADOWITZ IS a licensed clinical social worker, and is a licensed teacher in New York State. She holds a master's degree in education and one in social work. She has worked and volunteered for over thirty years in hospitals and nonprofit agencies in New York and California. She has experience in a wide variety of fields, including suicide and crisis, death and dying, drugs and alcohol, and developmental disabilities. Since returning from Louisiana Annette began working in the field of Family and Children's Service. Her interest continues to be in promoting healthy families. She is a member of the National Association of Social Workers and has recently been given the region B NASW Stand Up for Others Award.

Order Form

I would like to order additional copies of
Katrina: After the Storm

Name: _____

Mailing Address: _____

_____

E-Mail Address: _____

Quantity: _____   x $13.99 each: _____
Sales Tax: $1.15/8.25% (CA only):   _____
Shipping & Handling ($3 per book):   _____
Total Due: _____

Send check or money order to:

Annette Ladowitz
Clemson House Publishing
P.O. Box 2575
Saratoga, CA 95070-0575

Or e-mail aladowitz@gmail.com
for payment by credit card through PayPal

For presentations, book signings, and/or more information,
please contact the author, Annette Ladowitz, at the address
above or via e-mail at aladowitz@gmail.com.